MW01055025

UNDER GROUND

A FIREFLY BOOK

Published by Firefly Books Ltd. 2016

Copyright © 2016 Copyright Éditions

All rights reserved. No part of this publication may be reproduced, stored in a retrieval system, or transmitted in any form or by any means, electronic, mechanical, photocopying, recording or otherwise, without the prior written permission of the Publisher.

First printing

Publisher Cataloging-in-Publication Data (U.S.)

Names: Zerdoun, Catherine, author.
Title: Under ground : subways & metros of the world / Catherine Zerdoun.
Description: Richmond Hill, Ontario, Canada : Firefly Books, 2016. | Includes bibliography. | Summary: "The book is divided in 2 chapters. The first one focuses on the history of the subway in 6 cities (Paris, London, New York, Berlin, Moscow and Tokyo). The second chapter is an overview of the most remarkable and amazing subway stations around the world through 50 photographs, each one displayed on a double page" — Provided by publisher.
Identifiers: ISBN 978-1-77085-811- 4 (hardcover)
Subjects: LCSH: Subways — History. | Subway stations - Pictorial works.
Classification: LCC TF845.Z473 | DDC 625.42 - dc23

Library and Archives Canada Cataloguing in Publication

Zerdoun, Catherine, author
        Under ground : subways & metros of the world / Catherine Zerdoun.
Includes bibliographical references.
ISBN 978-1-77085-811-4 (hardback)
        1. Subways. 2. Subway stations. I. Title.
TF845.Z47 2016   388.4'2   C2016-900898-3

Published in the United States by
Firefly Books (U.S.) Inc.
P.O. Box 1338, Ellicott Station
Buffalo, New York 14205

Published in Canada by
Firefly Books Ltd.
50 Staples Avenue, Unit 1
Richmond Hill, Ontario L4B 0A7

Printed in China

Translation: Christine Schultz-Touge

Created by **Copyright Éditions**
104, boulevard Arago
75014 Paris – France

Original concept Capucine Viollet
Editorial director Laura Stioui
Editor Claudie Souchet
Artistic director Émilie Greenberg
Layout artist Nicolas Marchand
Copyediting & proofreading
Sabine Kuentz & Brigitte Balmes
Photoengraving Cédric Delsart
Production Stéphanie Parlange
and Cédric Delsart
Contributing authors Jean-François Pitet and Sylvie Deraime

UNDER GROUND

Subways & Metros of the World

CATHERINE ZERDOUN

FIREFLY BOOKS

table of contents

history of
the subway

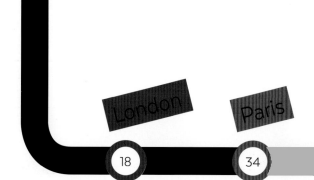

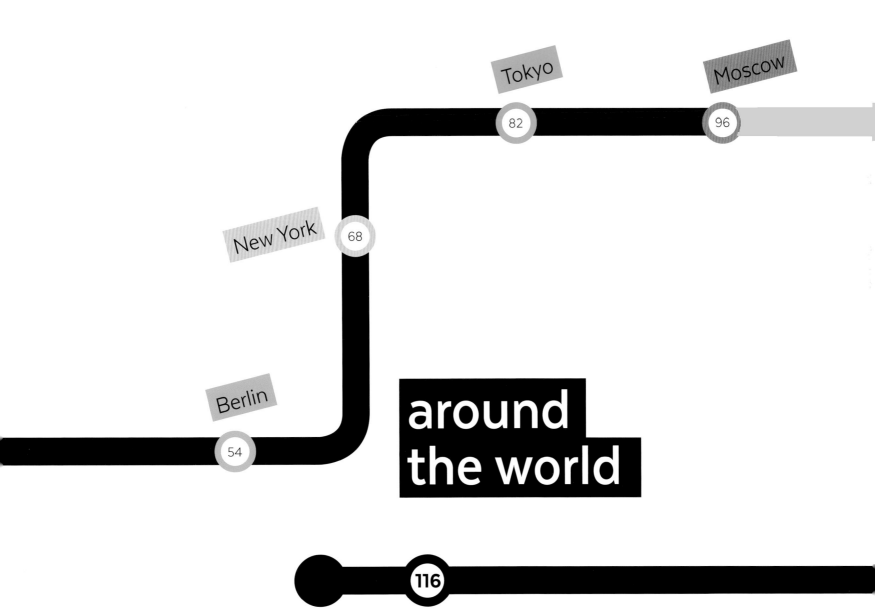

Tokyo 82

Moscow 96

New York 68

Berlin 54

around the world

116

A ticket to ...
rediscover the subway!

Wandering through the world's subways

For most city dwellers, the subway is first of all a means of transport, to go from point A to point B. But the subway can also be a place where you feel all sorts of emotions, when you meet the love of your life, or when a couple separates on a platform... In the same way, if we take a closer look around us, the world of the subway reveals its treasures: over a century of history, works of art and technological prowess... This everyday experience made up of smells, sights and sounds can become an unforgettable adventure when the hazards of chance, a glance or a delay, upset a journey.

This book, which presents the subway as you have surely never seen it, invites you to (re)discover this underground (and sometimes elevated) world all over the planet, and perhaps right next door to you.

Yesterday's subways, tomorrow's subways...

The main mission of every subway network has always been to keep traffic moving at street level and to manage city expansion, but it would be a mistake to think that these were the only purposes. Beyond economics and urban planning, the ambitions of the authorities heading these projects were often political, symbolic or cultural.

While each new subway, in order to to dig its route, must invade a space that doesn't really want it, once it has opened, it becomes an indelible part of the infrastructure, the landscape, the spirit of a city. It becomes a basic right, a symbol.

Around the world today, especially in China and India, new subway networks are under development and will soon see the light of day... by going underground.

Engineers, architects, workers and artists will need to, once again, skillfully work together to meet feverish urban expansion and build new stations, imagining new technologies, to be always faster, more fluid, safer...

"Even if you are alone in the subway, you are never lonely."

Anonymous

The train is about to depart—stand clear of the doors!

Let's go down into the subways of Paris, New York, Tokyo, London, Moscow and Berlin. Rediscover the romantic beauty of the Parisian stations, the thundering labyrinth of the New York subway, the artistic wonder and secrets of Moscow's Moskovsky Metropoliten, Tokyo's incredible *chikatetsu*, which is regulated to within a second, the underground scars of the Wall in Berlin's U-Bahn…

We'll stop, from station to station, to appreciate the ingenuity of the technicians, artists, architects, graphic artists and even the taggers! A discovery that is truly worth the price of a ticket!

You are about to take a very long journey...

The 10 longest subway networks in the world

While the oldest networks were dug in the mid-19th century, new subway stations open each week all over the world, implementing new technologies, meeting new ambitions. Ultramodern, efficient and fast, these networks, however, inevitably become quickly saturated, just like the car traffic at street level they were meant to relieve...

584 miles (940 km) - Seoul, South Korea

290 miles (467 km) - Shanghai, China

288 miles (463 km) - Beijing, China

249 miles (401 km) - London, England

228 miles (367 km) - New York, United States

204 miles (328 km) - Moscow, Russia

201 miles (323 km) - Tokyo, Japan

182 miles (293 km) - Madrid, Spain

144 miles (232 km) - Guangzhou, China

135 miles (217 km) - Paris, France

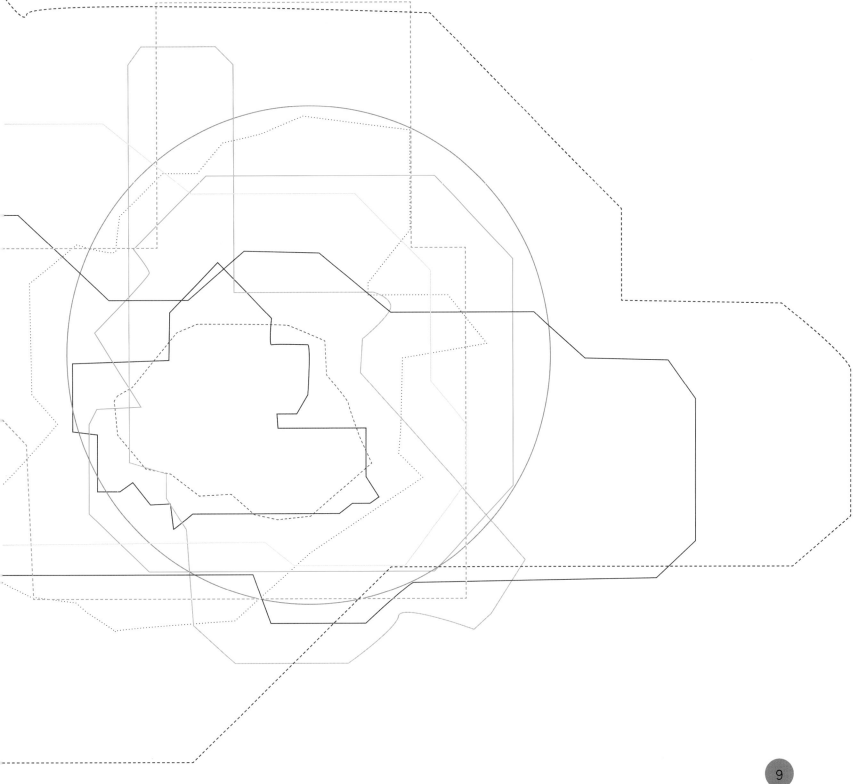

Building the subway
from 1863 to now

At first it was the traffic jams that pushed authorities to attempt to reduce street congestion with the help of public transport. In 1855 two engineers, Brame and Flachat, imagined a network connecting the market of Les Halles, Paris, to the periphery, in order to more quickly and easily transport merchandise – not people! The subway would not take long to go beyond its utilitarian beginnings to become a prestigious element and sign of modernity for cities.
This is shown by the regularity of new network debuts each year, nearly everywhere in the world.

1

London
January 10, 1863
Uncomfortable, suffocating, yet 40,000 Londoners happily traveled the 4 miles (6 km) of the first line opened between Bishop's Road (now Paddington) and Farringdon Street.

2

Chicago
June 6, 1892
One of the oldest elevated trains in the world, that residents call the "L" or "El" for "elevated."

3

Budapest
May 2, 1896
Completed for the millennium celebrations of Hungary's founding, it was the first European network that operated with electricity from the start.

4

Glasgow
December 14, 1896
A single peripheral line of 64.6 miles (104 km), that has not been modified since its opening.

5

Boston
September 1, 1897
The Boston "T" as the locals call it, was the first underground network built in North America. When it opened, many tramway lines were closed in order to decongest the city center.

6

Paris
July 19, 1900
Political divisions, personal interests and endless debates between the city and the national government, delayed the first project that dated from 1855. The Universal Exhibition of 1900, organized in Paris, forced everyone to finally agree on the inauguration date.

7
Berlin
February 18, 1902
An elevated train that first ran a short stretch in the city. It should be added that an urban railroad already existed at the time.

8
New York
October 27, 1904
Elevated, steam, cable-drawn or pneumatically powered, there were already many railroad lines in New York when the subway opened. And the ancientness of some structures that still exist shows that they were made to last, but also that it is urgent to modernize them.

9
Tokyo
December 30, 1927
The late arrival of the railway in Japan partly explains the late opening date of its capital's subway. It was, however, the first subway in Asia and at the time covered a distance of only 1.4 miles (2.3 km).

10
Moscow
May 15, 1935
Even if the first Moscow subway project goes back to 1902, it was the exponential growth of the city's population that pushed Stalin to resume work in 1931.

11
Isfahan
October 15, 2015
This is the most recent arrival, with only 10 stations spread over 6.8 miles (10.9 km), pending completion of the network which should cover 26.7 miles (43 km). Isfahan is the fourth Iranian city where people can travel by subway.

Subway stories
Anecdotes, historical events, records...

**With millions of passengers each day, the subway is obviously the scene of amazing situations, both happy and sad. And some popped up very soon after the debut of the subway.
Today, between musical performances, historical events, flash-mobs and other happenings, not a day passes without riders having a story to tell. Here is a sample.**

15 the number of diamonds lost in the New York subway

...on the day of its inauguration, on October 27, 1904, by the third person to have bought a ticket that day. The 15 diamonds, totaling 1 carat, were on a horseshoe brooch that a woman wore purposely for the occasion (value at the time $500, or about $15,000 today).

45 the number of ghost stations in the London Underground

These ghost stations are scattered throughout the network, and are no longer used for various reasons: insufficient ridership, transformation into a shelter, modification of the network... In Paris, there are 11 stations which have been permanently closed to the public and two that were built but never opened!

21 h 49 min 35 s the fastest time to travel through all of the stations of the New York subway system

This record is held by Matthew Ahn, a young law student, since January 16, 2015 and earned him a place in the Guinness Book of World Records.

4 **the number of times that Queen Elizabeth II of England has gone down into the Underground**

During her visit in 1969, on the occasion of the debut of the Victoria line, she even drove a train for a few stations! Her last trip goes back to 2013 during the celebrations for the 150th anniversary of the London Underground.

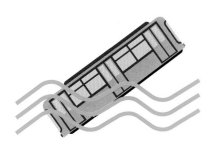

714
the number of cars from the New York subway that lie underwater

In 2008, 714 red cars from the New York subway were sunk off the coast of Slaughter Beach in Delaware in an amazing recycling campaign. The goal? To create an artificial reef that was named Redbird Reef. No one asks the fish for their tickets, honest.

O **the number of snacks allowed in the Caracas subway**

Don't try to bring your snack into the subway of the Venezuelan capital: at each station entrance, a specially designated security guard verifies that you have nothing to eat in your hand.

1642 **the oldest subway tunnel dates from that year**

More specifically, it is the vault of a sewer built during the reign of Louis XIII and discovered by workers when digging the Châtelet-Pont-au-Change station in Paris. They thus took advantage of the preexisting work, which can still be seen today.

The subway, by numbers
London, Paris, Berlin, New York, Tokyo, Moscow

While Parisians often claim that "métro-boulot-dodo" (subway-work-sleep) sums up their daily life, and New Yorkers complain of the "rat race" (literally, since the rodents swarm in the subway), we must also spare a thought for Beijingers, who, during each rush hour, must relive the nightmare of record-breaking shoving and squeezing! But the billions of passengers transported every year probably do not know these incredible numbers.

16

subway lines
(including **2** secondary,
or "bis" lines) in Paris

430

escalators, with
23 at Waterloo
station, inside the
London Underground

469

subway stations, of which
60% are underground in
New York

563

subway trains in service
during rush hours in Paris

10 subway lines in Berlin

13 subway lines (plus the Yurikamome automatic elevated line) in Tokyo

40 stations form the longest subway line in Berlin (the U7, from Spandow to Rudow)

11 subway lines in London

9,715,635 passengers on December 26, 2014: a record ridership in Moscow subway

12 subway lines in Moscow

24 subway lines in New York

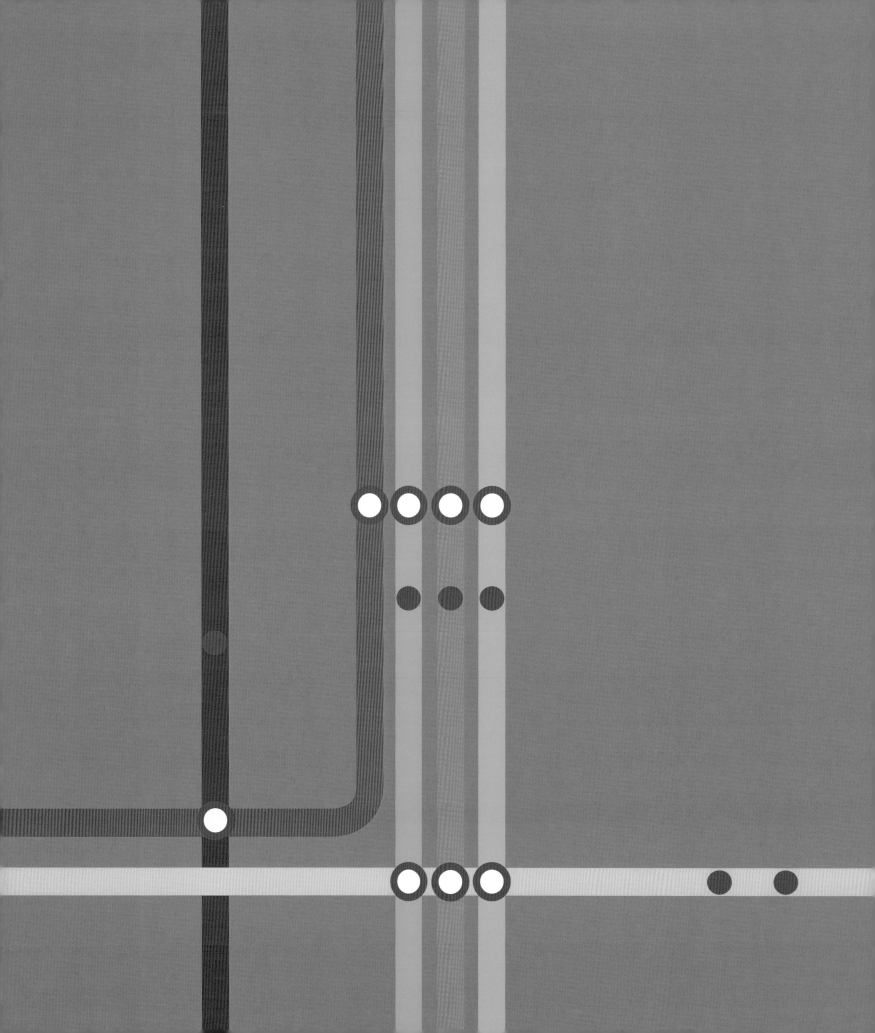

history of the subway

london

Mind the gap

Expensive, packed, often uncomfortable and not always reliable, every day the London Underground transports more than 3.5 million passengers who complain about it but can't live without it! This venerable system, which celebrated 150 years of operation in 2013, truly defines the outline of the city, connects it, keeps it alive. It is also the cornerstone of the largest metropolitan area of Europe (606 square miles/1,570 sq. km and 8.5 million residents), which could not exist without its excellent transport network. A veritable engineering marvel, which was at the cutting-edge of progress on many occasions, the London Underground also played a social role in democratizing access to the city. Its unique modernity and aesthetic have contributed to giving a strong identity to the United Kingdom's capital. In the 21st century, as for all of the world's subways, it must meet new challenges, among which security and reliability take first place.

"The Tube"
The London Underground

"Who would dare to venture into the ignoble underground of London, in its dark and noisy tunnels . . . in its corridors infested with rats, soaked with discharge from sewers, polluted by fumes from the gas ducts?"

1863
THE DEBUT OF THE LONDON UNDERGROUND

C. H. GRAVES, PUBLISHER AND GEN'L MANAGER PHILADELPHIA, U. S. A.

SOLD ONLY BY AGENTS OF

THE UNIVERSAL PHOTO ART CO.

7506 Ludgate Hill, London

This is what an editorialist from the very respectable British daily *The Times* wondered in 1862. According to him, even if the construction of the subway seemed possible from a technical point of view, the undertaking was doomed to failure: no one would use it! A few months later, on January 10, 1863, some 40,000 curious people who crowded into the Paddington train station for the inauguration of the first line of the Metropolitan Railway of London, proved him wrong: they boarded, delighted, for an 18-minute journey taking them to the Farringdon railway station, eight stops away—a trip whose duration has not changed much since. Thus after two decades of debate and three years of construction, London opened the first underground transport network in the world.

The world's largest city

In the mid-19th century, the capital of the powerful British Empire was the largest city in Europe with over 3 million inhabitants when Paris had only slightly more than one million inhabitants, New York, 810,000, and Berlin around 520,000. This great industrial metropolis was also home to the busiest port in the world. Yet its geographical organization remained very archaic, experiencing unparalleled population densities with many of its residents subjected to deplorable living conditions. The steam train, born in Great Britain in the 1820s, was already part of Londoners' daily lives.

A station in the 1890s. The wooden platform floors proved especially slippery in rainy weather!

Dense traffic at Ludgate Hill in the City area. Every sort of transport crowded the neighborhood's narrow winding streets. It was high time that the Underground was opened...

270

STATIONS, OF WHICH 55% ARE UNDERGROUND.

↓ Construction at Notting Hill station in the 1950s.

Every day, some 725,000 passengers got off in one of the capital's four major railway stations, from which they had to find a means of reaching their workplace . . . by foot, omnibus, horse-drawn tramways or by boat. At one point Parliament refused to allow train lines to extend any further in London.

The visionary Charles Pearson, a solicitor and once a member of Parliament, who had campaigned in favor of trains in the city since 1845, believed that trains were the only solution for decongesting the city. When he presented his plan for an underground train, the municipality finally agreed with him.

From steam subway...

In 1860, Pearson created the Metropolitan Railway Company to raise funds from private investors to carry out his project. The first underground train line was built using the "cut and cover" method, which consisted of digging a rather shallow trench, installing two rails and covering it all with a brick structure. The construction created chaos wherever it occurred and forced the displacement of hundreds of residents. After attempts to move the train car using compressed air, the company wisely chose to use steam. The Metropolitan closely resembled a train. It offered different classes, and first-class passengers, who paid more for their tickets, boarded before the others.

But the pollution generated by the steam locomotives proved unmanageable and travelers often came out of the underground a bit grimy and half asphyxiated.

...to electric underground

However, the means of transport quickly became indispensable to them. Some 11.8 million Londoners rode it the first year. Other lines managed by various private companies were were quick to emerge,

Stockwell subway station in south London. Debuted in November 1890 by the Prince of Wales, future Edward VII, it was one of the deepest on the network and the southern terminus of the City & South London Railway.

such as the Metropolitan and District Railway (1874) which, in 1884, opened a circular line, which is still the Circle Line today. With the expansion of the network, other means of tunneling appeared, such as the shield perfected by the South African engineer, James Henry Greathead, which made it possible to dig tunnels in relative security for the workers and deep enough so as to limit disturbance at street level. The apparatus was gradually moved forward during excavation, while a lining of cast iron segments was progressively fitted on the tunnel walls.

But the greatest innovation was the appearance of electric locomotives, which in 1890 made the London subway the first of its kind. At the time, only tramways ran by electricity, and the engineers working on the City and South London Railway had to face a real challenge! The equipment was placed in a small locomotive fueled from a power station. But the line experienced distribution problems: the further the train went from the Stockwell station, toward the end of the line, the more unreliable its power became. And passengers were often plunged into darkness.

The American Influence

In 1900, the Central London Railway in turn launched a line. It crossed the city from east to west and had the distinction of introducing the single-fare ticket, which earned it the nickname of Twopenny Tube. The idea came from the United States, as did the General Electric locomotives, which arrived in component parts, and the use of a third rail, which placed between the two exterior rails, provided the supply of electricity. It was at this same time that Charles Tyson Yerkes made his entry onto the scene. This American financier, whose reputation was tarnished by several scandals, had participated in the development of the Chicago subway. He brought American technology and capital to London and bought several lines with the plan to unify the network but also to give it a strong identity within the urban landscape. For the technical side,

→
The entrance to Hammersmith station, in southwest London. It is located at the junction of three different lines.

he acquired the gigantic Lots Road power station, at the time one of the world's largest. For the aesthetic side, he called on the architect Leslie Green, who designed 11 stations between 1904 and 1906, including Mornington Crescent and Gloucester Road, still recognizable today at first glance due to their oxblood-red tiled façades and their very Arts & Crafts details.

A subway that redefined the city

In 1905, Yerkes's Underground Electric Railway controlled all of the lines in London with the exception of the Metropolitan and the Waterloo & City. Frank Pick, who was company executive, took charge of its development and of its visual identity and graphic design. It was his idea to write the name of station in white letters on a blue enamel rectangular plaque placed on a red disk and then, later, on a white disk circled in red. This circle and this bar became—and still are today—the symbol of the London subway, which as of 1908 would be called the Underground or, more familiarly, the Tube, because of the rounded shape of its tunnels and stations. Pick was also behind an especially well-designed advertising campaign, which if it did not directly praise the subway, reminded Londoners

of all the places it could take them: the theater, movies, shopping: "Think of the Underground!" Probably even more than elsewhere, the Underground had redefined the city's geography. By extending its lines far beyond the center of London as of 1880, it encouraged the development of suburbs and the decongestion of certain neighborhoods. Killing two birds with one stone, the concessionary companies developed urbanization projects near the lines they were building, giving rise to a veritable "Subway-land." Thus, residential areas such as Wembley Park, Harrow Garden Village and Kingsbury Garden Village were connected to the city center by subway!

On the eve of World War II, the London Underground enjoyed the reputation of being simple and functioning well. In the 1920s, sliding doors had been installed in the cars to facilitate the boarding and unloading of passengers. Until then an employee had opened and closed doors at each end of the car. In the same concern for efficiency, a conductor's cabin was added to each end of the train: it was no longer necessary to change the loco-

A conscientious subway: notice boards in the stations were at the disposal of riders who could leave their suggestions, comments and complaints (1922).

Gants Hill station on the Central Line. This stop, serving the borough of Redbridge in northeast London, was designed in the 1930s by Charles Holden.

motive when the train arrived at the end of a line, instead the conductor would change cabins.

In 1923, the architect Charles Holden designed new stations, which were built using modern materials, such as concrete, and geometric shapes recalling constructivism. In 1933, riders were able to find their way through the subway more easily thanks to the the first schematic map designed by Harry Beck (1902–1974) which also served as a model for the creation of subway maps in all of the world's major cities. The same year, the London Passenger Transport Board, a public company, unifed the network.

A concert at the Aldwich station during World War II: one of the few distractions organized by Civil Defense to support the morale of Londoners severely tested by the German bombing.

Take cover!

In 1940, during the Blitz, when German bombs were plummeting down on London, 79 of the network's deepest stations were transformed into shelters. At each alert, and often during the night, thousands of people found refuge on subway platforms converted into dormitories. As during World War I, women replaced men in many functions: they were in charge of subway maintenance and worked in various workshops, especially for weapons, set up underground. Even the government found refuge in the subway: the disused Down Street station once hosted the War Cabinet of Prime Minister Winston Churchill. From August 1940 to July 1941, more than 40,000 explosive bombs and several million incendiary bombs beat down on the city, causing incalculable dam-

age and the death of over 40,000 people. Some had found refuge in the underbelly of the capital. The Underground's biggest disaster, however, had nothing to do with bombings: on March 3, 1943, after a false alarm, a panicked reaction in the escalators of Bethnal Green station caused the death of 178 people. This was such a horrific event that the government censored it until the end of the war.

To feed the subway refugees, refreshment trains operated two times each day, late in the evening and early in the morning before service started again. Hostesses got off to offer drinks and snacks on the platforms: nearly a thousand people were mobilized to prepare and sell products.

3.5
MILLION DAILY PASSENGERS

Modernization at record speed

Postwar times were all about reconstruction and modernization. By 1953, wooden cars had entirely disappeared. New aluminum trains, inspired by the fuselage of war planes, began to operate: they were 20% lighter than those made of steel, were not subjected to rust and therefore did not need to be painted, representing a savings of two tons of paint per car. As of the mid-1980s, however, they would be painted in the subway's colors of blue, white and red to discourage recurrent graffiti.

In 1969, the Tube was again front-page news for being the world's first line having automatic pilot. On March 7, Her Majesty Queen Elizabeth II debuted the Victoria Line, on which the conductors needed to only close the doors and switch two buttons to start the train, which if the tracks were clear, would then run at a controlled speed to the next station before coming to a stop. That same year, users could buy their transport tickets from automatic vending machines: the tickets were then equipped with a magnetic strip to be read by automatic gates, which were also brand new... Since 2003, tickets have almost disappeared, being replaced by the Oyster Card, a contactless smartcard, in which credit and passes can be stored.

Perplexity... Newly arrived immigrants from the British Antilles try to get their bearings on the subway map. They don't know what they owe to the ingenious Harry Beck, the industrial designer behind the schematic (and simplified) map of the complex London network, still in use today.

↑
The Tube as it looks today.

The subway of the future

Since the 1980s, lines have never stopped being modernized while extending into new areas.

In 1987, the subway network added that of the DLR (Dockland Light Rail), with which it allows connections. Tied to the rehabilitation of the docks neighborhood, this light rail, mainly elevated, serves the east of the city. Its logo is similar to that of the Underground, but a turquoise circle takes the place of the red one.

Overground stations, in operation since 2007, can be recognized by their orange circle. This transport network, mainly on the surface, which covers Greater London and the county of Hertfordshire, is a suburban rail network that also crosses the city and has connections with the Tube. In 2018, three Crossrail lines will be added. This express rail network will also serve Greater London. These various means of transport, as well as buses and the like, are all overseen by Transport for London (TFL), a local government organization created in 2000.

Today, certain lines run around the clock on weekends, are air conditioned, have platform edge doors for safety and offer Wi-Fi. Riders will soon have access to real-time information, and new more ergonomic cars are being evaluated. The world's oldest subway is facing the challenges of the 21st century.

paris

It's so much a part of the physical and mental landscape, of the some 12 million riders in the Parisian urban area, that they barely notice the subtle century-old decorations that are scattered through their subway system and are often unaware of the technical prowess that was needed to construct this 135-mile (217 km) subway. While at the dawn of the 20th century, Paris was later than other major metropolises, when the city did open a subway in 1900 it was electric from the start, mostly underground, and was part of a coherent plan to serve the capital. It was nearly completed on the eve of World War II. The distance between stations has increased along with the number of lines, but it remains one of the world's shortest—1,600 feet (500 m) on average—for a network of this length. The billion and a half passengers who take the RATP trains each year are always ready to grumble when an incident or strike disrupts traffic. Yet they benefit from a well-performing service and the most recent technology, for example, the automatically driven trains that are set to conquer Grand Paris.

The Paris Métro
An unconditional cultural symbol

In 1881, the International Electricity Exhibition, organized in Paris at the Palais de l'Industrie on the Champs-Élysées, honored the magical energy that lit up Thomas Edison's light bulbs and drove Werner von Siemens's tramway. However, seven years later, the French capital, which showed such great enthusiasm for technological progress, was just beginning to electrify. And the major works undertaken during the reign of Napoleon III did nothing to help: to circulate through the busy streets of Paris was a nightmare. When there was no more room on the crowded omnibus, which was often, the only choice was to suffer the rude manners of cab drivers and be armed with patience. To cross the city could take hours. The Universal Exposition of 1889 threw a cruel light on the delay that Paris suffered when it came to urban transport.

French engineers, however, were not short of ideas for endowing the capital with a subway that was worthy of it. Since 1845, the projects had piled up, such as one for a subway circulating on inclined planes, thanks to the pull of gravity, between central Paris and the Gare de Lyon and Gare du Nord, or the project, proposed in 1888 by Jean-Baptiste Berlier, for an east-west subterranean tramway, between the Bois de Vincennes and the Bois de Boulogne.

The Palais des Nations, built for the Universal Exhibition of 1900 would receive 51 million visitors. It was vital to establish service worthy of the event.

Municipal councilors did not want an elevated train, like the Elevated in New York, which would disfigure Baron Haussmann's magnificent perspectives. In the country of Pasteur and concern for hygiene, the idea of a train spewing black fumes was also very unpopular. Fortunately, electricity could now solve the problem. Yet the debate continued. The major rail companies insisted that the entry of trains into Paris be to their benefit: they wanted a Parisian network that connected with the national train stations. The national government agreed with them. But the city councilors resisted, fearing that such a network would encourage an exodus of Parisians to the suburbs, and also that they would find themselves tied up and bound by these powerful companies.

Construction, in 1905, of the Passy bridge, crossing the Seine, seen from the Grenelle station–today Bir-Hakeim–on Line 6.

1900
THE DEBUT
OF THE PARIS MÉTRO

Fulgence Bienvenüe, with cane and white beard, during the inauguration of the extension of the current Line 8, for the Colonial Exhibition of 1931.

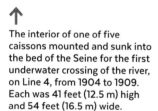

The interior of one of five caissons mounted and sunk into the bed of the Seine for the first underwater crossing of the river, on Line 4, from 1904 to 1909. Each was 41 feet (12.5 m) high and 54 feet (16.5 m) wide.

Bienvenüe, chief engineer of a major undertaking

The approach of the Universal Exhibition of 1900 called for an end to procrastination. The national government gave in and the city council finally voted, on November 22, 1895, for the construction of an exclusively Parisian subway. The operation of it was granted to the Compagnie du Chemin de Fer Métropolitain de Paris (CMP), founded by Baron Édouard Empain. But the city was in charge of the cost and implementation of the immense construction project, overseen by Fulgence Bienvenüe. After attending the École Polytechnique he had worked as an engineer at the Ponts et Chaussées and constructed rail lines in the west of France before being recruited by the city of Paris, where he finished Haussmann's water supply program and designed Belleville's funicular tramway.

↑ →

When not perforating tickets, punchers would often shout across the platforms to chat with colleagues.

His project for an electric metropolitan was declared to be of public utility in 1898. He planned a 40-mile (64 km) network built around an inner circular line and two transversal lines, one east-west, the other north-south. The lines would be independent, with no section in common, and the trains would stop at every station: the rider would thus not need to verify the destination of the train arriving in the station. From the outset Bienvenüe had devised a coherent and dense network: wherever they might be, Parisians would find a station no more than 1,300 feet (400 m) away and they would never need to make more than two connections, whatever their route.

Work on the first line (segment of the present Line 1) intended to connect the Porte de Vincennes, on the east, to Porte Maillot, on the west, started in February 1899 and advanced at a rapid pace. Rue de Rivoli was ripped up in order to dig the trenches, which were then repaved in order to build an underground tunnel at a shallow depth. The process was cheaper and faster.

The two thousand mobilized workers still accomplished an amazing feat. They finished 6.8 miles (11 km) of tracks and eight stations in 16 months. When the line was debuted, on July 19, 1900, the Universal Exhibition had already been open for three months. The event did not make the newspaper headlines and no government minister even bothered to come.

All aboard on the first line: from Vincennes to Porte Maillot!

As for the travelers, they showed up from the start. In the fall, the 10 other stations of this first line, with two branches under the Place de l'Étoile—one toward the Bois de Boulogne, where Parisians enjoyed strolling, the other toward Trocadéro and the Universal Exhibition—were all opened. By the end of 1900, 17 million little cardboard tickets had been sold by the agents posted in the ticket hall of each station, which gave access, according to an unchanging plan, to a hallway leading to two lateral staircases, on either side of the tracks. At the bottom, the ticket puncher would grab the magic voucher and with a skillful stroke, punch a little hole in it. The cunning and the poor quickly learned the art of filling in the hole with a breadcrumb to travel a second time for free, thus fooling the vigilance of the virtuoso puncher, who worked in relative darkness.

Le Petit Journal

Le Petit Journal
CHAQUE JOUR — SIX PAGES — 5 CENTIMES

5 Centimes SUPPLÉMENT ILLUSTRÉ 5 Centimes
Huit pages

ABONNEMENTS

Le Supplément illustré
CHAQUE SEMAINE 5 CENTIMES

L'AGRICULTURE MODERNE, 5 cent. — • — La Mode du Petit Journal, 10 cent.

SEINE ET SEINE-ET-OISE 2 fr. 3 fr. 50
DEPARTEMENTS 2 fr. 4 fr.
ÉTRANGER 2.50 5 fr.

Quatorzième année   DIMANCHE 23 AOUT 1903   Numéro 666

TERRIBLE CATASTROPHE DU MÉTROPOLITAIN
Découverte des premiers cadavres

Yet, for the time, the Paris subway was not that poorly lit. The light was amplified by the white or opalescent ceramic tiles that covered the walls and surprised those who were expecting a dark and dirty décor, like everything else underground. The trains, with cars made of wood, were more rustic. Passengers could only trickle through their single-wing doors. Their opening and closing was controlled by the conductor, for whom a seat was reserved in the front motor car.

Soon it was necessary to increase train frequency: during rush hours, it went from 10 to 6 minutes, then to 3 minutes in 1901.

Fire at the Couronnes station: lessons from a historic catastrophe

A second line, semi-circular and in part elevated, was soon opened between Bagnolet, to the northeast, and Porte Dauphine, to the northwest (segment of the current Line 2). It was on this line that on August 10, 1903, the worst catastrophe in the history of the Paris Métro occurred. A fire had broken out under a motor car as it approached the Barbès station. The passengers were evacuated, the fire put out, and the empty train continued to the terminus. But the fire restarted at Ménilmontant. The electrical wires run-

The catastrophe at the Couronnes station, on August 10, 1903, recalled major mining tragedies and revived fears linked to the underground world. Yet the fatal fire would promote the arrival of a truly modern subway.

303
SUBWAY STATIONS IN PARIS

ning through the tunnels melted, and the line was plunged into darkness. A train full of passengers stopped at Couronnes. The CMP guards urged the occupants to get off and leave the station. Many refused, demanding reimbursement of their tickets. The smoke forced them to comply, but then they panicked and there was a stampede toward the only exit: 84 people lost their lives.

This tragedy, which made headlines worldwide, momentarily caused a 40% drop in ridership. The CMP quickly reacted. From then on each station must be equipped with a clearly marked exit at each end of the platform, as well as a fire station and an emergency post. Electrical installations were assessed. Finally, long before the railroad companies, the CMP adopted metal rails with bogies—mobile axles allowing the train to better navigate curves—on which the electrical materiel was isolated. No more fatal accidents were to be tolerated on the Paris subway, excepting what are euphemistically referred to as "rider's accidents," referring to falls onto the tracks, whether voluntary or not.

Nord-Sud trains were more modern from the start: they had two motor cars each bearing two 125-horsepower engines. A train of five cars thus ran at a commercial speed of 13.7 mph (22 kmh).

The Paris subway counted 48 million passengers over about 8 miles (13 km) in 1901. In 1939, 800 million traveled on a network covering 69.6 miles (112 km).

The second, elegant network

From the start the Nord-Sud (North-South) flaunted its difference with brightly colored cars—red and yellow for first class, shades of blue for second, as opposed to the drab gray and green of the CMP cars. The refined rotunda of Gare Saint-Lazare displayed the desire of Jean-Baptiste Berlier, the founder of the Société de Chemin de Fer Électrique Souterrain Nord-Sud de Paris, to combine efficiency and a sophisticated look. Travelers mingled at Saint-Lazare where they would take one of the two lines, opened respectively in 1910 and 1911, whose stations with friezes in colorful faïence broke with the monotonous sanitary white. Station names were shown on blue tiles surrounded by a green border, rather than enamel plaques. Destinations of the trains were indicated over the arched entrances of the tunnels. One served Line A in the north-east/southwest direction, from the Porte de la Chapelle to Issy, via Saint-Lazare and Montparnasse stations (currently Line 12); the other served Line B, connecting Saint-Lazare to Porte de Clichy or Porte de Saint-Ouen (currently a section of Line 13), the fork at the La Fourche station going against the principle of the independence of lines so dear to Fulgence Bienvenüe.

4.18
MILLION DAILY PASSENGERS

Challenges facing the Nord-Sud network

Despite the skepticism of Bienvenüe and the opposition of the CMP, Jean-Baptiste Berlier managed to convince the Paris council of the feasibility of deep tunneling, thus freeing the subway from following the route of the street above. Associated with the financier Xavier Janicot, he pledged to be responsible for all of the construction. In 1901 he obtained a concession for three lines that were declared to be of public utility in the following years, which would allow riders to go from one network to the other using the same ticket.

Preliminary surveys, however, revealed that it was impossible to dig below the water table. And even moving the tracks upward was problematic—the climb toward the Butte Montmartre was a technical headache and a money pit. From the Notre-Dame-de-Lorette station, it was necessary to create a long slope increasing by ½ inch per foot (4 cm/m) and following a 18.5-foot (5.6 m) radius curve. The platforms of the Abbesses station ended up at 102 feet (31 m) below the surface: an elevator was indispensable. It was doubled by a helical staircase with two flights of stairs, allowing the circulation of two separate flows of riders.

In spite of a continual increase of ridership, the Nord-Sud network would never be able to balance its budget. The depleted company would be absorbed by the CMP in 1930.

The first Seine crossings

The challenges were no less daunting on the network operated by the CMP. Between 1903 and 1904, the Austerlitz viaduct was built over the Seine (for the current Line 5). The metallic construction of the only Paris bridge reserved for the subway had to be free of pillars so as not to interfere with navigation. To support the 279-foot (85 m) deck, suspended from parabolic arcs spanning the river for 459 feet (140 m), it was necessary to sink foundations at 33 feet (10 m) below the average water level.

On September 2, 1939, France declared war on Germany. The Madeleine station was closed to the public, who were directed to that of Opéra.

Another challenge was the line connecting Porte de Clignancourt, in the north, to the Porte d'Orléans, in the south (currently Line 4). Opened by sections from April 1908 to January 1910, it required making the first crossing under the Seine. Five enormous steel caissons were mounted, some on the Quai des Tuileries, right bank, others at Place Saint-Michel, left bank, before being "sunk" to more than 49 feet (15 m) deep in the riverbed.

→
The RER (Regional Express Network) was launched on July 6, 1961, with marketing fanfare: it would, however, take 16 years to finish Line A, which doubled Line 1 of the subway.

Where it intersected with the Chemin de Fer d'Orléans (currently Line C of the RER), the saturated ground had to be frozen by means of pipes filled with brine, so that a tunnel could be dug connecting the caissons on each side. The construction lasted four years, during which workers toiled under the water, in a chamber filled with pressurized air, communicating with the surface by telephone.

1920s: The subway extends throughout Paris —and beyond

In 1910, the first network imagined by Bienvenüe was completed, but with 365 million riders per year it was already insufficient. Construction of two new lines began, including one that linked Porte de la Villette and Pré-Saint-Gervais, to the northeast, with Opéra (currently segments of Lines 7 and 7 bis). Passing through the former gypsum quarries of Buttes-Chaumont, the construction once again required engineering prowess. Under Place du Danube, the foundations were set 115 feet (35 m) underground. The subway system stretched throughout Paris in the 1920s. Its lines were extended since the poorest Parisians, driven from the center by rising rents after World War I, had moved to the working-class suburbs on the periphery. By early 1929, its 15 lines (of which 2 were secondary, or "bis" lines) running 70 miles (113 km), were taken annually by some 800 million travelers. At the end of the year, the general council of the Seine department voted for the extension of the network to the inner suburbs, where individual houses were spreading. While the old "fortifications" were replaced by the Boulevards des Maréchaux, the Métro ventured beyond the city limits, toward Pantin, Les Lilas, Charenton, Levallois and Neuilly; it stretched over 99 miles (159 km) to serve an agglomeration thathad gained nearly 1.5 million inhabitants between 1900 and 1930.

1939-1945: The Métro keeps running

On September 2, 1939, while France was preparing for war, the subway closed some of its stations for the first time in its history. Some, like Arsenal, would never reopen. During the first month of the "phony war," service was reduced by 40%. But the Paris buses having been requisitioned by the army, the subway absolutely had to run. During the calamity of spring 1940, it evacuated soldiers and civilians night and day. When Paris was occupied by the Germans, with rationing of gasoline and tires, it maintained a vital link. At the closing of theaters and cabarets, everyone rushed to catch the last subway before the curfew.

When the sirens sounded, Parisians sought shelter in the stations; tunnels sometimes served as secret meeting places for Resistants. During the night of April 20 and into the morning of April 21, 1944, allied bombs fell on the workshops of the du Saint-Ouen subway; they caused the death of over 200 civilians. But the Métro kept running, only completely stopping between July 22 and 30, then again from August 6 to 12, 1944.

→
A disheartened crowd on the former Nord-Sud line.

It was still running at the Liberation under the supervision of an interim administration of Parisian transport, precursor to the creation, by a law of May 1948, of the Régie Autonome des Transports Parisiens (RATP), a state-owned industrial and commercial company.

1950-1970: Slow modernization

The RATP inherited a network, which after having figured among the world's most modern, seemed aging and old-fashioned in the interwar period. The installation of neighborhood maps, telephones, candy and soft drink vending machines on the station platforms was not enough to boost its image. At a time when the car was becoming king, the subway had to modernize, despite a chronic lack of funds. In 1952 the first renovation of stations using *carrossage* (sheaths of metal paneling) began and would be financed by advertising: at the Franklin D. Roosevelt station, a painted metal covering rose halfway up the vaults. Seventy-three stations would soon be sheathed.

At the same time, new trains dethroned the iconic Sprague ones (the first train cars made entirely of metal): in 1951 articulated, modular trains appeared in blue and cream; in 1957, a new material on tires, making starting and slowing down more efficient, thus increasing frequency of service, was launched on Line 11, between Châtelet, in the heart of Paris, and Mairie des Lilas. But now a new competitor arrived on the scene: in 1961 construction was launched on the first east-west line, of the future Réseau Express Régional (RER), in order to facilitate the travels of suburban commuters. It would connect the new business district of La Défense, which was quickly breaking ground, to Place de la Nation, and decongest Line 1. Completed in 1977, the speedier Line A of the RER would accentuate the frustration of riders of the good old *Métropolitain.* "Métro, c'est trop," the group Téléphone sang that same year, giving voice to the feeling that riders had had enough.

The Parisian Métro entered into the 21st century with Line 14. Fully automatic trains run at an average speed of 25 mph (40 km/h) instead of 15 mph (24 km/h). Stations focus on open space, stone and glass.

A "chic and shock" renovation

The RATP tenaciously continued its modernization program. Train operation was now being automatically controlled from a central location—the station chief left the platforms to go up to the ticket halls. Equipped with a magnetic band since 1969, tickets were automatically controlled when riders inserted them into "tripods." The last ticket punchers disappeared in 1973, two years before the introduction of the Carte Orange, which was at first a monthly pass.

The large orangish tiles seen at the turn of the 1970s once again became a hygienic white a few years later and were outfitted with standardized furniture, making it an especially uncomfortable place for the homeless. Even so, in 1981, the subway came back into favor, thanks to a compelling advertising campaign: the "chic and shock" ticket with its brown band became trendy and truly democratic when the Communist Minister of Transport, Charles Fiterman, did away with the anachronistic first class. In 1983, President François Mitterrand debuted the driverless VAL de Lille. Paris would also have its entirely automatized subway on Line 14, which the huge tunnel-boring machine, Sandrine would begin to drill in 1993. This line, on which trains run two times faster, was inaugurated five years later between the Madeleine station and the new Bibliothèque Nationale, before being extended to Gare Saint-Lazare to the north and the Olympiades station to the south, in the 13th arrondissement. Ironically in the history of transports, this line had partly been designed to relive the RER A.

A great subway for Grand Paris

Having become the RATP showcase for exporting its expertise abroad, Line 14 is also one of the major axes of Grand Paris Express, a project approved in 2011 by an agreement between the national government and the Île-de-France region. This network serving the Greater Paris area will consist of four subway lines going from suburb to suburb, and the extension of two existing lines. By 2025, Line 14 should thus extend to the airports Roissy-Charles-de-Gaulle to the north and Orly to the south. By 2024, Line 11 will be lengthened to reach Noisy-le-Grand to the east and Rosny-sous-Bois to the northeast.

The Parisian subway network will thus double its scope and once again demonstrate its capacity for evolution that has never faltered, while serving development policy projects for Paris and its suburbs as well as the comfort of its residents.

The fabulous history of the Guimard entrances

On June 10, 1899 the newspaper *L'Architecture* announced the terms of a competition launched by the Compagnie du Métropolitain Parisien (CMP) for the design of *édicules* (kiosks) to decorate and identify the street entrances to the future Parisian Métro. Since some city council members from the bourgeois neighborhoods in the west refused that an overly visible urban structure disfigure the stately Parisian avenues, it was understood that these would be "constructions as elegant as possible, but especially very light." There would not be any on the Champs-Élysées nor before prestigious monuments such as the Opéra. None of the projects presented would see the day after the rejection of the proposals made by architects accredited by the CMP. Hector Guimard, one of the "most revolutionary of Parisian architects," was then called upon. Equally functional and audacious, his "Chinese pavilions"—which would be installed at Place de la Bastille and Place de l'Étoile—his "dragonfly" *édicules* and especially his canopies, in cast iron and glass, are ranked in the inventory of Historic Monuments, since 1978. But it was not until the 1990s that a complete restoration campaign was financed. It demonstrated the attachment Parisians have to the framed entrances, the plantlike wrought iron and glass canopies, now so associated with the poetic charm of *Amélie Poulain*'s Paris in the minds of foreign tourists.

→ The very rundown "Chinese pavilion" of the Bastille station, was destroyed in May–June 1962.

→ An old railing with escutcheons at the George V station: 68 of these railings, familiar to Parisians, are still in place. The map support is not by Guimard. These did not appear on the Parisian network until 1913.

346. PARIS — Station du Métropolitain - Place de la Bastille   E. L. D.

When, in 1996, the yellow trains of the Berlin *Untergrundbahn* once again crossed the Oberbaumbrücke, over the Spree River, a painful chapter of the city's division—and that of the entire country—came to a close. The U-Bahn, like all transport from 1945 to 1989, had been at once both a tool and a witness of the Cold War; as with Berlin, an impassable wall cut it in two starting in August 1961. During the Belle Époque, being among the most innovative of the early subways, it had confirmed the modernity and the grandeur of the German Empire's capital when faced with the rivals of London, Vienna and Paris, shaping what would become Greater Berlin in 1920. Reunited and modernized, today its 10 lines—serving a capital city of 3.5 million inhabitants—stretch over 344 square miles (891 sq. km—eight times the area of Paris), the European Union's second city, which never stops reinventing itself.

Reunified city, reunified subway

berlin

The Berlin U-Bahn
A subway for an imperial capital

When on February 18, 1902, the first section of the Berlin subway, connecting Stralauer Tor to Postdamer Platz entered into service, Berlin already had an urban train, the *Stadtbahn*, that crossed the city from east to west, via the historic center of Mitte, along with a number of electric tramway lines. The inventor of that highly urban mode of transport, Werner von Siemens, had imagined, as of 1880, giving Berlin a subway like the one London already possessed. He died 10 years before Hochbahngesellshaft, a subsidiary of the Siemens and Halske company, which he had founded, undertook the construction of the first Berlin line, extended in 1902 up to Warschauer Brücke and the Zoologischer Garten.

Berlin, the capital of Prussia, which became the capital of the German Empire in 1871, had over one million residents in 1880. At the dawn of the 20th century, although it was a major railway crossroads, travel within the city remained difficult. The first subway line was quickly adopted by the public and soon the neighboring communities of Charlottenburg and Wilmersdorf to the west, and of Schöneberg to the south, decided in turn to establish a line

The major part of the first Berlin subway was elevated. Between Warschauer Brücke and Gleisdreieck, the current U1 runs on a viaduct overlooking the Landwehr Canal.

connecting with Berlin's center. By 1906, it was possible to travel up to Richard-Wagner-Platz in Charlottenburg. This town, which was home to the royal residence since the 18th century, had insisted that the extension of the first line up to the zoo should be underground, which established the fact that it was possible to dig tunnels underneath Berlin. As for the city fathers of Schöneberg, they imposed their subway against the wishes of Wilhelm II, who opposed service to that part of Berlin.

Developing the subway in 1920s Greater Berlin

In 1913, the city-state of Berlin launched the construction of a north-south line: this would be the first large-gauge line, allowing the circulation of wider and higher train cars than on earlier tracks. Work was interrupted by World War I. Despite the considerable difficulties faced by the defeated Germany, the line was completed in 1923. Three years earlier, the Weimar Republic had founded Greater Berlin, which annexed seven neighboring towns,

1902
THE DEBUT OF THE BERLIN SUBWAY

In spite of the heavy war reparations that Germany had to pay to the victors of World War I, German industry recuperated in the 1920s. The opening of the Berlin municipal subway in 1923, reflected this recovery.

Finely crafted lights and clocks
at Wittenbergplatz station.

including Charlottenburg, Wilmersdorf and Schöneberg, 59 communes and 27 rural districts: the capital's surface area was increased by tenfold and its population rose to nearly 4 million inhabitants. In "Roaring Twenties" Berlin, at once a cultural beacon of Europe and an industrial center, the expansion of the subway continued, under the supervision of Ernst Reuter, director of transportation for the Berlin government as of 1926. In 1929, this last initiated the creation of a large municipal transport authority, the BVG, resulting in the fusion of public tramway, bus and subway companies, which made a unique urban transport tariff possible, and democratized public transport.

Grenander, the unique style of the U-Bahn

Starting in 1902, another man, Alfred Grenander, left his mark on the Berlin subway and the capital's architecture. Head architect of the subway company, he drafted the plans for many viaducts and train stations, which today still account for half of the network. Considering industrial design to be an inclusive work of art, Grenander invented train stations where every element, from the signage of the entrance buildings, to the lighting was integrated into the whole at the start of

1,142

TRAINS IN SERVICE
IN THE BERLIN SUBWAY

the design process. From Jugendstil, the German equivalent of Art Nouveau, to industrial functionalism, he explored every style, including Neoclassicism. At Wittenbergplatz, Berlin's first station, rebuilt between 1911 and 1913 to accommodate five platforms, he also constructed an impressive theater. Hermannplatz station, created between 1923 and 1927, was the first to be equipped with escalators, connecting the two platforms built one above the other. It also was given an entrance directly into the Karstadt department store, which had just been opened. While architecturally remarkable, Grenander stations are also easy to spot thanks to their distinguishing colors: yellow ceramic tiles at Hermannplatz, blue-gray ones at Alexanderplatz, which is home to Berlin's first underground shopping center. Rainer Rümmler, who would design all of the U7 line extension, in the 1970s and 1980s, would respect the principle, while imposing his own style: Bayerischer Platz displays the blue and white of Bavaria, while Paulsternstrasse sparkles with stars ("stern" in German).

Grenander designed Wittenbergplatz station at the beginning of the 1910s. The yellow mosaic is one of the architect's major features.

U2 ▸Ruhleben

Potsda

← Ausgang   **i**

Leipziger Platz
Leipziger Straße

← Ⓜ M48
🅑🅤🅢 200, 347

– eine

Berlin Year Zero: in 1945, the former capital of the Reich was largely destroyed. One-fifth of the housing was uninhabitable and the infrastructure needed to be rebuilt: the subway was hardest hit by Allied bombing.

West Berliners flocked to the Friedrichstrasse station in 1964. A pass allowed them to catch a train or an S-Bahn to reach the East so as to visit their families on the other side of the wall.

Reconstruction was started immediately after the capitulation of the Third Reich. In a city in ruins and largely depopulated, hundreds of thousands of women (at the time there were five for one man!) cleared the rubble, with the means at hand, under the supervision of Soviet soldiers, who alone occupied Berlin until the end of June 1945. While half of the tramway lines were back in service by the end of 1945, and the S-Bahn (suburban trains) were repaired in 1948, the last reconstruction work on the U-Bahn was not completed until 1951.

Dividing the subway

Now governed by a special statute, Berlin, occupied by four victorious powers—the Soviet Union, the United States, the United Kingdom and France—became the epicenter of the Cold War during which the Communist bloc and Western liberal democracies would clash. And transportation was one of the nerve centers of the war. From 1945, the Soviets had taken control of the S-Bahn. It did, however, continue

to circulate between the occupied zones, as did the U-Bahn and tramway. Tens of thousands of Berliners traveled to work from East to West, and vice versa, every day. The blockade of the Western sector, imposed by the Soviets, from June 1948 to May 1949, did not interrupt this circulation; it was, however subject to heavy controls by the police from the East. It continued after the proclamation of the Federal Republic of Germany, on May 23, 1949 (the German Democratic Republic was born on October 7) and after the split of the BVG, on August 1, 1949, induced by the Soviet command following the crisis caused by the general strike of S-Bahn workers. The assets of the BVG were divided: the BVG of West Berlin, where two of the three million Berliners lived, obtained the major part of the U-Bahn lines; the BVG of East Berlin, which would be renamed BVB (for Kombinat of Berlin transports), received Line 5 and the eastern part of Line 2.

The tests of war

The Great Depression and then, in 1933, the rise to power of the Nazis, brought a sudden stop to the subway's expansion. Like in Paris and London, during World War II, its underground areas served as shelters during bombing, which caused enormous destruction as of 1943. During the last weeks of the war, there was fighting in the tunnels. In early May 1945, German troops set off explosives in the subways, thus hoping to slow down the inexorable advance of the Red Army. The waters of the Spree rushed in, a third of the tunnels were flooded, and hundreds of Berliners who had taken refuge there were drowned.

Outside Potsdamer Platz
station, soldiers and civilians
climb the wall to watch how
is life on the other side, in 1961.

"Freedom for the price of a U-Bahn ticket!"

The citizens of East Berlin, which became the capital of the GDR in defiance of the quadripartite status of 1945, could still ride the entire Berlin transport network. An increasing number took a one-way ride toward free-

dom. The West German press encouraged them: "Freedom for the price of a U-Bahn or S-Bahn ticket," they openly repeated.

Between June and July 1953, however, interzone traffic was completely stopped for a month, during the People's Uprising in the East, which was violently suppressed

by Soviet tanks. Afterward, controls became more drastic in the border stations of the East. Signs and loudspeakers warned riders when they were arriving at the last station of the Western sector. Yet at the Friedriechstrasse border station, where the dreaded Stasi operated alongside the transport and customs police, the flow of emigrants did not ebb. Each year some 200,000 fled Communist Germany.

The Wall, on the surface and… underground

At midnight on August 12, 1961, by order of the GDR's Minister of the Interior, all trains running on the East side were stopped. Passengers were forbidden to get off the until their identity and zone of residence were verified. At street level, East German armed forces blocked the roads and the railways leading to West Berlin. In the following hours, they began to erect a wall that would permanently separate families and friends, enclosing East Berliners and isolating those of the West as if on an island. At the same time, tramway and S-Bahn rails were removed, and the U-Bahn stations leading toward freedom were walled up.

Lines 1 and 2, going in the east-west direction, were cut. The circulation of the meridian lines 6 and 8 serving West Berlin neighborhoods, passing by East Berlin, would be reestablished but under the conditions of the GDR. The BVG-West had to pay very high rent to its Eastern counterpart for the use of it rails and tunnels. The trains were forced to slow down when approaching the closed stations of East Berlin: they passed at reduced speed before platforms that now held only uniformed men, whose mission was to prevent,

day and night, escapes through the underground network. To prevent the soldiers themselves from defecting, they were quartered in bunkers built on the platforms of these ghost stations.

A startling before and after! After the fall of the Berlin wall, Nordbahnhof station was rebuilt at the exact same location as it was before the wall was erected.

In the West, the automobile

While the subway, too expensive, fell into to disuse in East Berlin, which by contrast extended the tramway, it was favored by West Berliners, who were called by Willy Brandt, the mayor-governor of the city from 1957 to 1966, to boycott the S-Bahn, which had fallen into the hands of the GDR. The Berlin Senate decided to extend the U-Bahn network. Lines 6 and 8 were lengthened; Line 9, which avoided East Berlin, became the new north-south line.

1.38
MILLION DAILY PASSENGERS

The bus network was also developed, but it was the car that triumphed, like in all Western cities. West Berlin constructed urban expressways.

From "reunified" subway
to tomorrow's subway

When in the early evening of Thursday November 9, 1989, after months of protest in the East, the authorities of the moribund GDR announced that the citizens could now cross the Wall, a flood of pedestrians and Trabants went West. Underground, the

U-Bahn participated in this extraordinary celebration: it ran all night long. And the next day, the Jannowitzbrücke ghost station was reopened: Line 8 was once again connected with the major lines of the East's S-Bahn. Other stations, closed for nearly 30 years, quickly came to life.

But the service in reunified Berlin did not live up to its new status. The BVG, which absorbed the BVB in 1992, since West Germany had integrated the former East Germany two years earlier, became a vast redevelopment project, while the city-state of East Berlin was almost bankrupt.

The work was never ending. First of all, the networks between the East and West had to be balanced. Some stations closed, others opened, while new lines appeared. In 2010, the BVG started a new landmark project, expected to be completed in 2017: to link the U line to Line 5 between Friedrichstrasse and the avenue Unter den Linden. Three stations were to be created: Unter den Linden, Museum Insel and Berliner Rathaus, in order to make the historic center of Mitte and the German capital's tourist attractions more accessible. The subway is contributing, again and as it has before, to the reinvention of Berlin.

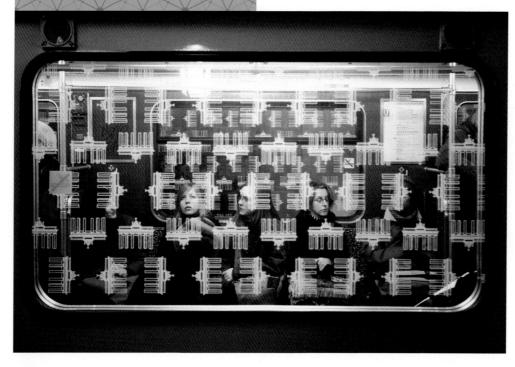

On certain subway lines, the trains' windows are decorated with engravings representing Berlin's most remarkable monuments. Here it is the Brandenburg Gate.

new york

The Subway, the American way

With over 1.7 billion passengers in 2014, the New York Subway is the leading subway in the United States. In world ranking, it sits in 6th place in terms of ridership frequency, after Tokyo, Moscow, Seoul, Shanghai and Beijing, but before Paris, Mexico and Hong Kong. It's not especially beautiful; it's not particularly clean; it's not very comfortable in spite of the air conditioning; it is even so noisy that experts advise passengers to wear earplugs to protect their hearing while traveling, due to the 80 decibels (on average) to which they are exposed—by comparison, a chainsaw emits 100 decibels... New Yorkers have a strange love-hate relationship with their subway since it is as indispensable as it is insupportable! Like all older networks, the New York Subway is at a turning point in its history.

The New York Subway
A means to connect boroughs

In 1898, New York adopted a new administrative organization, which gave birth to the city as we know it today: New York County (Manhattan), Bronx County (the Bronx), Kings County (Brooklyn), Queens County (Queens) and Richmond County (Staten Island) were combined to form Greater New York, divided into five boroughs. This change of scale called for new infrastructures equal to the immense metropolis of 3.4 million inhabitants, the largest in the country, and the world's second largest city after London.

In the mid-19th century, the most outlandish projects flourished to try to resolve the increasingly crucial problem of transport in the city. One of them, for example, envisioned an elevated rail system with a steam locomotive on top and cars suspended by their roofs underneath it, so passengers would not be bothered by fumes. Another proposal to decongest the streets was to to install giant conveyor belts overhead, fitted with benches and cabins so that passengers could seek cover in case of bad weather... In a city where the trolley represented the major means of public transportation, the circulation was so bad that

Faster and cleaner than a horse-drawn carriage, less expensive to build and easier to maneuver than the cable car, the electric trolley was long favored by New Yorkers. The development of individual vehicles marked the start of its decline.

The New York metropolitan area
at the end of the 19th century.

a columnist for the *New York Tribune* ironized that it would take less time to travel half way between New York and Philadelphia than to cross Broadway, the busiest street of the city! Why did it take New York so long to develop modern transportation when the technology and the capital were available? The answer lies in three words: William Magear Tweed (1823–1878). A particularly corrupt politician and the third-largest property owner in New York during his heyday, "Boss Tweed" supported the street-level transport lobby and used all of his energy to fight against subway projects, whatever they might be.

The El weaves its web…

Tweed, however, could not oppose the opening, during the summer of 1868, of the first elevated train line, designed by the engineer Charles Harvey and composed of cable-drawn tramways, preceding by five years San Francisco's cable cars. Nor could he do anything to stop pneumatic subway test runs born from the fertile imagination of Alfred Beach, in 1869. Developed below the ground of the most congested section of Broadway, the system included a tubular car with 22 places, propelled in a tunnel of several hundred feet by a gigantic 1,000-horsepower steam blower. Despite the enthusiasm of the passengers and the success of the process, Beach had to abandon his project

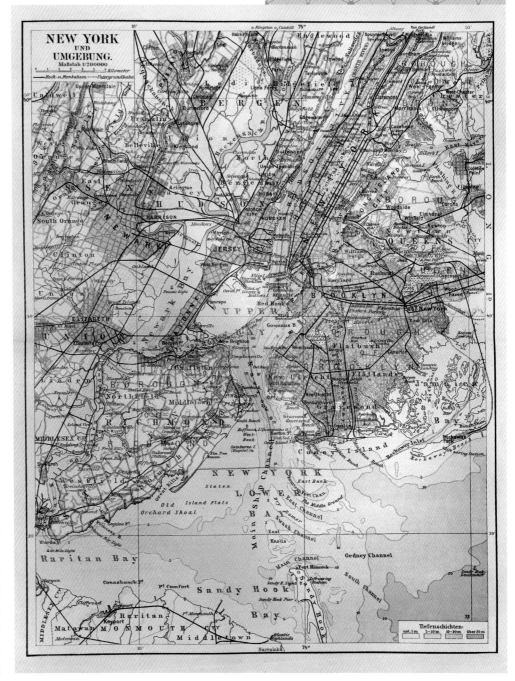

El lines in the south of Manhattan: the Bowery (below) and the Lower East Side (facing), going to the Brooklyn Bridge. In spite of its many inconveniences, this means of transport faithfully served New Yorkers for 76 years.

when faced with resistance from politicians and financiers... Meanwhile other elevated lines, or "El" lines, were developing somewhat chaotically in various parts of the city, especially in Manhattan and Brooklyn. At the time northern Manhattan was an undeveloped area, so it posed no problem, but in the lower part of the island, the noisy elevated trains darkened the streets and were not appreciated by all of the residents.

Their extension, however, helped to push the city limits: farmland became suburbs, suburbs became neighborhoods, and New York ceaselessly expanded. By the end of the 19th century, however, in spite of all its lines, the El, converted to electricity thanks to its third rail, had not solved the problem of transport in the heart of the city.

...And the subway digs in under ground

The project of a subway was then underway and was something New Yorkers could hardly ignore, given the havoc that it caused during construction. In March 1888, an exceptional snow storm had para-lyzed the city for over two weeks and the idea of underground transport generated new interest. The scheme envisioned by Abram S. Hewitt, the city's mayor, was original: instead of resorting to the usual formula of concessions, he wanted to separate the ownership of the land and lines, which belonged to the municipa-lity, from the construction and financing of lines, granted to private companies. The business community and building promo-ters were against it, and it was finally the financier August Belmont, representing the Rothschilds in the U.S., who was awarded the rights in 1900. The Interborough Rapid Transit Company (IRT) was established in 1904, the same year it opened its first line. The subway was built within the deadline, without going over budget or having any serious accidents, despite the use of dyna-mite to bore most of the tunnels.

COPR. DETROIT PUBLISHING CO.

12498   APPROACH TO BROOKLYN BRIDGE, BROOKLYN, N. Y.

1918

THE MALBONE STREET WRECK

Starting in 1913, the Brooklyn Rapid Transit Company, soon to become the Brooklyn-Manhattan Transit Company (BMT) built a second line. In the 1930s, a third group, the Independent Subway System (IND), financed with public funds, was born. Unlike the others, which set out to reach new neighborhoods, the IND worked to strengthen the existing network in the city center. Fiorello LaGuardia, mayor of New York as of 1934, attempted to reorganize subway infrastructure under the sole authority of the city: it was accomplished in 1940.

To each their car!

By the 1910s every area of the city was served by the subway, setting off housing booms, here and there, but during the 1920s, the focus has turned to individual travel. New York became an automobile city. There were some 2,400 cars in 1900; by 1920 the number had reached 213,000. The Williamsburg, Manhattan and Queensboro bridges made getting The Malbone Street Wreck around more easy; road infrastructures that allowed connections in the city and with neighboring states were increasing, encouraged by LaGuardia but especially by the urban planner Robert Moses, president of the New York State Council of Parks and the Long Island State Park Commission. So up until the 1960s, bridges and tunnels, parkways and

New York holds the sad record of the worst accident that ever occurred in subway history. On November 1, 1918, a Brighton Beach Line elevated train approached the Malbone Street Tunnel at over 40 mph (64 km/h), while the speed limit was 6.2 mph (10 km/h). The locomotive derailed and the two following cars jumped the tracks: 97 people perished, 250 others were seriously injured. The cause: the speed, of course, but also the inexperience of the conductor, a certain Edward Luciano, recruited hastily during a labor strike, and the obsolescence of wooden cars. All charges were eventually dropped and Mr. Luciano changed careers to real estate.

Brighton
Beach

BRIGHTON
BEACH
Ⓑ EXPRESS
MANHATTAN
& BRONX

4.53
MILLION DAILY PASSENGERS

→

Improvised underground concert. Musicians have only officially been authorized to play in the New York Subway since 1985.

highways were built, neglecting the subway. The city fathers were content to gradually dismantle the El structures, which disappeared in 1955.

The rehabilitated subway

At the end of the 1970s, the invasion of graffiti in the subway struck home with a message: New York was out of control. Yet it took over a decade until Rudolph Giuliani, the "zero tolerance" mayor elected in 1994, took things in hand. The subway gained in comfort—air conditioning, introduced on some lines in the 1960s, became widespread; maintenance was reinforced; efforts were made on cleanliness; the tiled décor in the oldest stations was renovated. The availability of Wi-Fi on the much of the network was announced for the end of 2016 as was the introduction of contactless smart-

cards, on which it is possible to store credit and passes, replacing the magnetic card in use since the disappearance of metal tokens in 2003.

Nevertheless, taking the subway in New York remains a real adventure for novices, because it's not always easy to find your way around. The lines, indicated either by number or by letters, sometimes use the same tracks and you must be very careful to get on the right train when waiting on a platform shared by several lines. You also need to pay attention to the way the name of the line is indicated on a train: if it appears in a circle it is a local or all-stops; if it appears in a diamond, it's an express train, which only stops at certain stations; in fact, the network has been designed from the outset in this spirit and some stretches of lines have four tracks, used respectively by the two types of trains. All of this in a deafening noise.

Graffiti: art or eyesore?

Urban phenomenon par excellence, graffiti (or tags) showed up in the New York subway in the 1970s. A new art form for some, a symbol of depravity for others, the phenomenon has always been fought by the municipality. The New York City Transit Police, even created a specialized unit in the battle against vandalism, the Vandal Squad, charged with arresting the perpetrators of "outlaw" painting. In 1989, after an eradication that cost $250 million, the last graffiti-covered car was removed from circulation. Since then, graffiti has entered museums where it has become a much less subversive art... It's interesting to note that major artists, such as Keith Harring and Jean-Michel Basquiat, started out by tagging the New York subway and its cars. But don't worry, tags can still be seen here and there in the subway!

→ In the 1980s, New Yorkers volunteered to clean the cars of their subways defaced by graffiti. The method may not be regulatory but the intention is good!

To the foreigner who takes it for the first time, the Tokyo subway seems at once familiar and bewildering. These are the same modern trains, the same underground hallways, the same magnetic passes as in the world's other subway networks. But here everything is multiplied and intensified: the *chikatetsu* shows the same excess as the Japanese capital itself. With its 13 lines covering over 186 miles (300 km), it forms one of the densest systems in the world, connected to a train network that is no less sprawling. Ridden by the 13 million inhabitants of intramural Tokyo and by some 40 million residents of the metropolitan area covering 3,025 square miles (7,835 sq. km—second in surface area after Greater New York but the most populated in the world), it should come as no surprise, that the *chikatetsu* is one of the busiest. Eight and a half million people ride it every day. Who would be amazed that it is so crowded? The miracle—very Japanese—is that it is so efficient and legendarily punctual.

A sprawling network

tokyo

Tokyo's *chikatetsu*
The miracle solution

In the early 20th century, Noritsugu Hayakawa, the "father" of the Japanese subway, spent hours posted at the intersections of Tokyo streets counting the number of trolleys and calculating how many passengers got on and off of them. At the time it was not uncommon, in this capital in full effervescence, that many frustrated people were left standing on the side of the road. There was not enough surface transport to meet the needs of two million residents already living in the city.

A view of the Ueno-Nakasendo train line from the Ueno station, in 1885. This would be at the head of the first Tokyo—and Asian—subway line, inaugurated on December 30, 1927.

1927
THE DEBUT OF THE TOKYO SUBWAY

Trained by Kaichiro Nezu, the "king of the rail," founder of Tobu Railways (now the second largest private railway company in Japan), Hayakawa was convinced that the solution to Tokyo's transport problems resided in the construction of a subway. Since the beginning of the Meiji era ("the renewal"), during which the former Edo became, in 1868, the capital of a Japanese empire in search of modernity, businessmen and engineers had been looking to the West for their models. Hayakawa, who was a bit of both, visited London in 1910. He came back filled with wonder for the Tube and energetically set out to persuade investors to rally around his great vision.

Hayakawa, a stubborn man

All of his interlocutors kept telling him: to bore subway tunnels was not possible under a city built partly on porous and seismic land. Hayakawa persisted. In addition to his ridership calculations, aiming to substantiate the project's merits and to deter-

mine the best route for the subway line, he also conducted geological studies. With figures and curves to support him he finally held a round table in order to found the Tokyo Underground Railway Company, of which he was first general manager before becoming its president, and obtaining a concession.

Construction work began in September 1925, two years after the great Kantô earthquake, which cost the lives of over 100,000 people in the great plain where Tokyo was located, which was ravaged by fires. On the subway worksite, obstacles accumulated: heavy rains flooded the tunnels; a major sewer was accidentally ruptured and under the pressure of the waste water that poured in, the steel rails bent like tin. After each inci-dent, Hayakawa would galvanize his troops of engineers and workers, reminding them that they were working for the country's economic growth and the well-being of their fellow citizens. On December 30, 1927, the first Asian subway line opened. The red and yellow trains running between Asakusa and Ueno were spacious, elegant due to indirect lighting, comfortable and made of metal. Wood, quick to burst into flame, had been rejected.

The 1930s and 1940s: a slow development

In 1931 this first line was extended toward the southwest up to Manseibashi, then up to Shinbashi in 1934. Hayakawa suffered a stinging setback when the extension of

It was at a crossroads like this that Noritsugu Hayakawa, the "father" of the Japanese subway, carried out his market studies: obviously, Tokyo was in great need of a metropolitan network.

→

Hall of the Shinjuku train station, where you can also take one of six subway lines.

the line toward Shibuya was assigned by the municipality to another company, the Tokyo Rapid Transit Company. In 1940, he was forced to resign following conflicts with shareholders. The following year, the two companies merged to form the Teito Rapid Transit Authority, which in 2004 would become the Tokyo Metro Co., whose shareholders were the Japanese national government and the Tokyo Metropolitan Government.

That same year of 1941, Japan officially entered the war on the side of the Axis against the Allied forces. Its economic investments were entirely devoted to imperialist expansion and victory.

The postwar boom

Put to its knees by two atomic bombs and under occupation, Japan recovered in the 1950s, experiencing an economic miracle that lasted into the 1980s. Tokyo was the motor. While the city, half destroyed by American bombing, was rebuilt without much regard for urban planning, stretching further out in an apparent chaos of large avenues and tangled alleyways, with always higher skyscrapers, the *chikatetsu* wove its web at an accelerated pace. The construction of the second line, that of Marunouchi, which crosses Tokyo from

northwest to east, began in April 1951. Like with the Ginza line that preceded it, the trains were powered by a third rail, running between the tracks at a standard gauge (1.435 mm). On the following lines, with a narrow gauge (1.067 mm), catenaries furnished electricity. In 1960, the Asakusa line, in the south-northeast direction went into service: it was operated by a new company, whose only shareholder was the Tokyo Metropolitan Government. The TOEI network (Japanese acronym of "Tokyo Metropolitan Bureau of Transportation") was extended with a second line in 1968. Meanwhile, Tokyo Metro (still Teito at that date) debuted two other lines and the first segment of the Chiyoda line opened in December 1969. The network then reached 62 miles (100 km).

The *chikatetsu* today: elegant, modern and spectacular

Tokyo Metro has, since then, doubled the size of it network, which now has nine lines and 167 stations. Currently the four lines of the TOEI network cover 75.5 miles (121.5 km) and serve 106 stations. One does not generally linger on the architecture of the Japanese subway, as if it is overwhelmed by the prestigious and imposing creations follow one after the other along its route. However, each of

the stations of TOEI's most recent line–Oedo, which started operating in the year 2000–have been designed by a famous architect. That of Iidabashi, designed by Makoto Watanabe, celebrates the evolving and organic architecture inseparable from Tokyo. Its singular forms were created digitally.

This is only one of the aspects of the *chikatetsu*'s modernity. On this same Oedo line, trains run with a linear motor. The Japanese subway has also adopted automatic control and command systems, which significantly reduce human error. There is no longer a conductor on the entire Yurikamome elevated line, which since 1995, links the artificial islands of the southeast to the Yamanote railway line, crossing the suspended Rainbow Bridge after a three-quarter turn. The view is breathtaking from the front of this first fully automated Tokyo train.

The subway attacked by the Aum sect

"The day is Monday, 20 March 1995. It is a beautiful spring morning ... You get up at the normal time ... and head for the subway station. You board the train, crowded as usual. Nothing out of the ordinary. It promises to be a perfectly run-of-the-mill day. Until five men in disguise poke at the floor of the carriage with the sharpened tips of their umbrellas, puncturing some plastic bags filled with a strange liquid..." recounts Haruki Murakami, in his novel *Underground*.

This liquid is sarin gas, a powerful nerve agent, invented by scientists working for the Nazi regime in the 1930s, and more recently manufactured by members of Japan's Aum sect. Five members spread out in five cars of the Chiyoda, Marunouchi and Hibiya lines, as they approached the stations Kasumigaseki and Nagata, located near the ministries and seat of the Japanese government. The attack caused 12 deaths and more than 5,500 people, riders and subway workers, were poisoned, including 50 very seriously.

The strategy of the Tokyoite rider

At stations on the five lines, platform edge doors now separate the tracks from the passengers who, during rush hours, line up in several rows while waiting for the next train. When it arrives, it's a compact but disciplined mass that rushes inside through the three large doors of each car. The image

5,400
TRAINS CIRCULATE EACH DAY ON THE NINE LINES OF THE TOKYO METRO CO.

Diligent and obliging, Tokyo subway guards are always ready to quickly and efficiently help fill the trains.

The Tokyo subway certainly reveals Japan's most modern side, where traditions survive against all odds.

of white-gloved station agents pushing passengers in by the back, so that the train can leave, sums up the insolvable congestion of Tokyo transport.

"When I say it's crowded, I was boarding a train once when my briefcase got swallowed up into the torrent of people and swept away. I was holding on, trying not to let go, but I just had to or my arm would have been broken," recounted one rider when interviewed by the writer Haruki Murakami for his book *Underground*. The trains, during the morning rush hour, run at double their capacity.

Each person has developed a strategy to adapt. There are those who have learned to sleep standing, some manage to be held up by their neighbors; others get

8.5

MILLION OF DAILY PASSENGERS

up at dawn to beat the crowd, calculating their route as closely as possible in order to catch a train that still has a few seats before the surge at major stations like Ikebukuro, a commercial and entertainment center, Shibuya, at the junction of the business district and Kabukicho's nightlife, and of course, Shinjuku, where a train arrives every 90 seconds.

The other Japanese miracle: Punctuality

Shinjuku, the world's largest station by surface area, and the first by ridership, has 10 floors and numerous exits giving access to several shopping centers. When a flood of passengers pours out of a suburban train and rushes to get on to one of six subway lines, it's futile to try to walk against the tide.

The Fukutoshin line, operated by Tokyo Metro, was debuted in 2008 to relieve the endemic congestion of transport on the section between Ikebukoro, Shinjuku and Shibuya, previously served by the private

rail company JR East. The subway passed the train!

Daily commuting, which often exceeds two hours per day for the average worker, might be stressful, but the *chikatetsu* guarantees getting to the office on time by avoiding the nightmare of automobile traffic.

Because in addition to being safe and of a cleanliness that would be seen as science-fiction in many other large cities, the Tokyo subway keeps it trains coming and going with a punctuality rate verging on 100%. It's almost an obsession for its agents. Those who establish the timetables

spend part of their time on the platforms observing the slightest perturbations that might disrupt the exactly timed choreography of the trains. For example, when winter is a bit harsher than usual, and passengers wearing bulky coats pile into the train cars a little less quickly, the train times will be adjusted by fractions of a second! Noritsugu Hayakawa's heirs watch over the fluidity of the underground ballet. This is probably the most surprising success of the *chikatetsu*.

The *chikatetsu*, a user's guide

As impressive as it might be at first sight, the Tokyo subway is fairly easy to get the hang of for those who read English, if not Japanese. Each of the 13 lines is identified by a letter and a color: G and orange for the historic Ginza line, for example. At the entrance to each station, above the ticket vending machines, an immense network map stretches out. It indicates, for each stop, the fare from the station where you are located.

The magnetic Suica or Pasmo card lets you avoid having to calculate the price of the ride. Valid on the subway, train and bus, the fare is debited when exiting at the end of the journey. Before the exit turns-tiles, there are machines for adding credit to a card, or for paying any balance owed, without surcharge.

To find the exit, other signs takes over. The only trouble is that the signage is sometimes interrupted when the route opens up into a shopping center... which is not unusual.

→ Subway map hanging above the automatic ticket machines.

→ Neighborhood map of Harakuju, served by the Yamanote railway line, of JR East, with connections for the Chiyoda line, operated by Tokyo Metro.

moscow

A Muskovite monument

A means of transport as well as a touristic curiosity, the Moscow subway will never cease to fascinate foreign visitors, just as it conquered the Soviet crowds astounded by a luxury that was new to them during its debut in 1935. Today, it still has the reputation as one of the most beautiful in the world, but also one of the most reliable. At any rate, it is certainly one of the busiest on the planet, and an unavoidable means of getting around this gigantic metropolis (over 386 square miles/1,000 sq. km, with more than 12 million inhabitants), whose boundaries are constantly being extended. Born during a very particular period of the city's and the country's evolution, the *Moskovsky Metropoliten* also represents a true slice of Soviet history and possesses a symbolic weight found in no other other transit system in the world. Welcome to an authentic Muscovite "monument"!

The Moskovsky Metropoliten
A socialist exploit

On May 14, 1935, the majestic Hall of Columns of the House of Unions in Moscow was decked out in the colors of the subway, which was scheduled to start running the next day. The day had been declared a national holiday. All the prominent figures of Soviet political life were there, beginning with Joseph Stalin, the leader of the Soviet Union. Lazar Kaganovich, second secretary of the Central Committee, minister of the railways, and first secretary of the Moscow Committee, had the honor of delivering the inaugural speech that he had titled, "The victory of the metropolitan is the victory of socialism."

Moscow in the early 1930s: traffic is heavy in the center of the capital, where there is still no subway.

The date of 1935 might seem surprising: how could a large city like Moscow, capital of the USSR since 1922, not have been equipped with a modern transit system much earlier, while London had its subway since 1863, New York, 1868, Budapest, 1896, Paris, 1900? Launched in 1931, the Moscow subway project that would eventually result, however, was not the first proposal. Two earlier projects, dating back to 1897, were never followed up upon by the municipality. In 1902, the engineer Balinsky submitted in turn an ambitious project to the Duma, the lower house of the Russian Empire: it called for the expansion of major roads, a passage underground in the city center so as not to disfigure historic neighborhoods and the construction of an elevated network elsewhere. Too expensive, it was rejected by the Assembly which preferred to develop the tramways already in operation. In 1912–1913, the question of city traffic became crucial: Moscow had over 1.6 million inhabitants, and the trams were saturated… At this time the subway became a serious consideration. But World War I broke out in 1914, then the revolution in 1917, followed by civil war which did not end until 1921… The subway was no longer on the agenda. Russia, then the Soviet Union in 1922, had to be (re)built.

Inauguration of the station Kolomenskaya, August 11, 1969. The opening of a new station was always an event celebrated with great pomp.

A Soviet achievement

As of 1923, however, a small engineering office organized within the Mossoviet, the municipality of Moscow, took a new look at the subject. In a country bled dry by recent events and lacking men who might have the necessary expertise, contacts were established with the German firm Siemens-Bauunion, which developed a very complete project including a circular line and several radial lines. Opinions were split: the capital had to face other emergencies, it lacked housing, hospitals, schools. It seemed preferable to continue to prioritize the development of surface transport. In 1931, the Party decided in favor of the construction of an underground subway "as the main means of solving the transport problem": Moscow would not achieve effective industrialization without efficient means of transport. Since 1928, the USSR had in fact started a major economic turnaround with collectivization in the countryside and massive industrialization of key sites.

A city on the verge of a nervous breakdown

At the time Moscow resembled a large village organized in concentric circles around a historic center dominated by the Kremlin, the seat of political and religious power since medieval times. The transfer of the capital to Saint-Petersburg by Peter the Great in 1712 had diverted investments in Moscow for two centuries. The city, having two million inhabitants in 1926, had more than three million in 1932. Between 1929 and 1933, the population had increased by 58%, but the housing stock by only 14%. All of these new arrivals, many from the countryside, lived in deplorable conditions in collective apartments or outlying neighborhoods devoid of infrastructure. More than 85% of the buildings had only one or two stories, only 42% were connected to the municipal water system, most streets were unpaved... To get around, Muscovites could take tramways, buses (as of 1924) or trolleys (as of 1933), all of which was very inadequate. Horses and carts could even still be seen on the streets! The city was on the brink of suffocation. It was intolerable for the inhabitants, intolerable for economic development, but even more intolerable in view of its status as the capital of the first socialist country in the world, headquarters of the Comintern, the Communist International. As such Moscow had to show the hostile world what a socialist state could do.

1935
THE DEBUT OF THE MOSKOVSKY METROPOLITEN

First challenges

Subway construction was thus part of a more general plan of urban changes that aimed to build the Soviet society. A means of collective transport in a collectivist society was also a symbolic matter. At the same time foundations were being laid that would lead to to the General Plan for the reconstruction of Moscow in 1935. The subway designers, unlike their Parisian counterparts, who worked in a city already redesigned by Haussmann, had to anticipate urban planning, which was being discussed at the same time. This was not their only problem. In September 1931, the Metrostroi, the organization responsible for the construction of the subway, seemed to be off to a bad start for ensuring its task, namely the construction of a subway line 6.9 miles (11.1 km) long with 13 stations that must be opened in the fall of 1934 for the anniversary of the Revolution. Pavel Rotert, its director, was surrounded by 24 collaborators and could only obtain 5,500 workers of the 12,000 that he had asked for. While he had estimated the need for 250 trucks for the first excavation work, he was given only 7 vehicles, one of which was not even working, 9 tractors and 400 horses...

Free rein to the regime

Fortunately for them, unlike their foreign counterparts, the engineers of the Moscow subway did not have to deal with local residents. In the absence of land ownership—everything belonged to the government—they were free to trace the route as they wished. The first line, Sokolniki-

→

An open work site in the heart of the city. Displaced buildings, gutted streets, disrupted traffic... In Moscow as elsewhere, construction of the subway did not go unnoticed.

Park Kultury, which followed a northeast/southwest axis, had to relieve the city-center streets and connect it to the train stations and major parks. After consulting with French, German and British experts, the Soviets opted for a rather deep underground system, since from the beginning, they also envisaged a military role for the network. This option, which made the displacement of utility pipes unnecessary, the consolidation of building foundations and the leveling of the ground, was more functional but also costlier and required trained personnel. Especially so, since the Moscow subsoil presented wide geological diversity and high instability due to the fact that it had many rivers and streams running through it. In fact, the first subway line would be a testing ground for every construction technique and diverse methods of excavation, depending on the soil, and would include stations fairly near to the surface as well as those dug more than 100 feet (30 m) deep. In the same way, the choice of having a central or lateral platform in a station was not a given, but would be decided case by case.

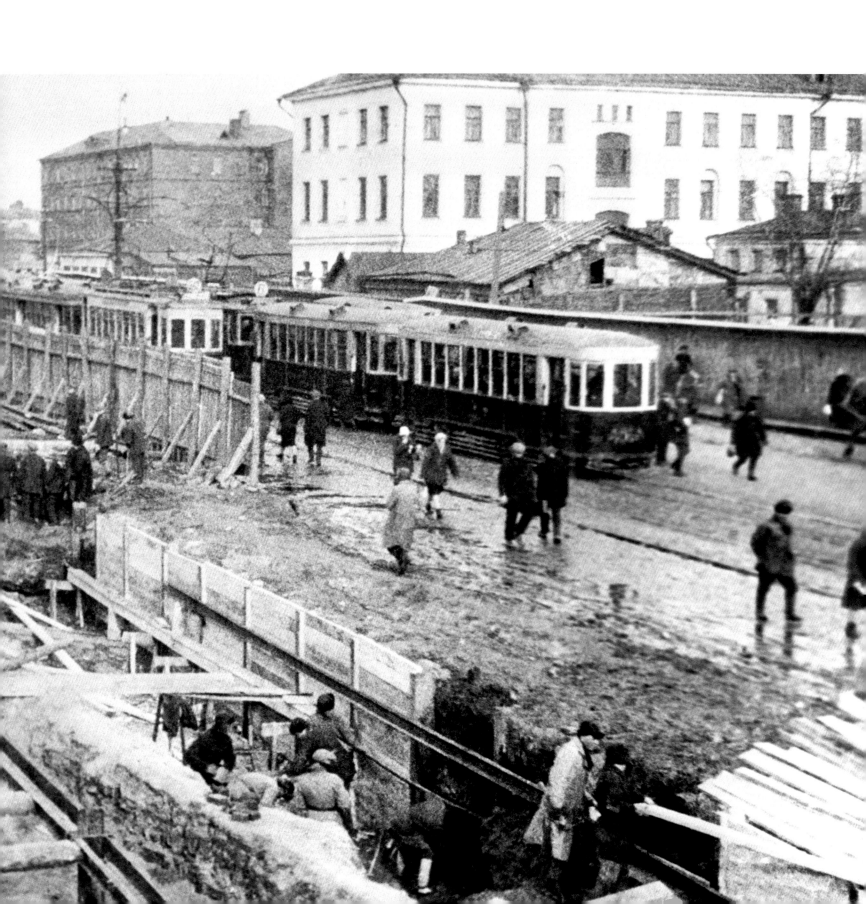

197
SUBWAY STATIONS IN MOSCOW

construction. A sponsoring system for various subway shafts was set up, to which the city factories contributed their equipment and workforce as part of the *subbotnik*, a program in which they worked "voluntarily" on Saturdays. "The entire country built the subway": the slogan was true, and it was through worksites like this that the "pioneer" spirit and the Soviet exploit mythology developed.

Authentic underground palaces

Just as important as the technical aspect, the aesthetic aspect of the stations was highlighted by the government. The subway's architecture had several missions to fulfill. It must educate the taste of passengers, instill them with optimism and confidence in a bright future: "Our worker who walks in the subway should feel happy and dynamic, because he knows that it is working for him, that each bolt is a bolt

"The entire country built the subway"

It was as part of the first two five-year plans (1928–1933 and 1933–1938) that the first stretch of the subway was completed. The workforce was one of the biggest worries of project. Entire villages of seasonal workers were hired and came to the Moscow region, but they also came from other Soviet republics where recruiters had been sent. These unskilled men were attracted by the opportunity of being housed and fed, even very precariously, and especially to obtain a *propiska*, a residency permit necessary to live in the capital. Farmers driven from

the countryside by famine also arrived in large numbers, but like most of the workers they were a very unstable workforce: of the 14,500 people hired in early 1932, only 5,500 remained by the end of the year. In 1933, the Komsomol, the Young Communist League, became a sponsor of the project: 13,000 young people of both sexes joined the ranks of the workers… but the clash of cultures with the "old-timers" was not easy. Working methods remained archaic. The poorly trained and poorly coordinated workers had only rudimentary tools such as shovels, picks and buckets. At the end of 1933, it was decided to requisition trucks from Moscow businesses, several times each month, to participate in the

Mayakovskaya station (1938), on the Zamoskvoretskaya line. Designed by Alexeï Duchkine (1904–1977), a key architect of the early subway and pioneer of the syntheses of arts underground.

of socialism." They should not have the impression of going down into the bowels of the earth nor the feeling of being oppressed. Beyond these laudable intentions, the rider should also feel humble and respectful in these stations of majestic appearance. Since it was a monumental, prestigious achievement, a symbol of the government's power and that of

Stalin, its leader, riches that came from the four corners of the country were put at the disposition of the subway, including vestiges of many religious buildings destroyed in Moscow and elsewhere after

the Revolution, such as the Cathedral of Christ the Savoir dynamited in 1931. Marble, an eternal material par excellence, was preferred, especially since it was easy to maintain. The government thus played a veritable role of patron, commissioning from the most famous artists and architects, from the finest sculpture, mosaic and painting workshops. This fabulous subway was a political declaration addressed to the Western capitalist world, by which it would demonstrate that the palaces could belong to the people, Communists, far from being barbarians, were the successors of a great culture and that the nation of proletarians was one of savoir-faire. Today, the subway décor reads like a picture book with a mix of figures and themes glorified at the time of the USSR. Workers, laboring alone, in a brigade or in a factory, play an important role: they constitute the basis of social order and without them the subway would never have come to be!

Their "doubles" are rural workers within a kolkhoz, an agricultural cooperative. Symbol of fertility, the earth is often associated with images of smiling and vigorous collective farmers. Women, in fact, play a major role in Soviet society since maternal figures guarantee family cohesion and, by

→
The entrance to the Krasnye Vorota station, opened in May 1935 on the first line of the network. The shell-shaped façade was designed by the architect Nikolaï Ladovski, known for his avant-garde work.

extension, patriotic cohesion... all the way to the embodiment of the Motherland, whose representations appeared during World War II.

A stylish subway

On May 15, 1935, after the opening date had been postponed two times, it was an awestruck public that entered into these underground palaces as if into a dream. The escalators, synonymous with modernity, made a very strong impression. Some stations were preceded by a vestibule but the practice was expensive and tended to disappear in favor of more simple entrances. The cars were decorated in the English style with longitudinal banquettes; great attention was given to the body of the car, ventilation and passenger comfort. Some stations, simple and functional, bore traces of waning constructivism, for example Miasnitskaya Vorota (now Kirovskaya), created by Nikolai Kolli, was remarkable for its lighting hidden under a cornice running the length of the vault. But it was the more monumental proletarian classicism, the "Red Doric" of Ivan Fomine, master of the genre, which triumphed in stations like Krasniye Vorota, whose entrance resembles a tunnel leading to a Neoclassical-style

underground hall, or Okhotny Ryad, a decorated station of Line 1—and the only one on the network to use imported material, silvery marble from Italy.

The trials of war

After the inauguration fanfare of the first line, the workers went back to their digging. The 1933 plan included the creation of 10 radial lines, later followed by two circular lines. These are the 12 lines of the current network, which however, have only one circular line, which mainly follows the Garden Ring, a succession of boulevards then on the city's outskirts. In March 1938, other stations were added to those of the first line, while the second line, Gorkovsko-Zamoskvoretskaya, following a northwest/southeast axis, was opened in September 1938. Plans for construction of a third line were put on hold during World War II, which the USSR entered in June 1941. Seven stations were nevertheless constructed during this period. As planned, the subway served as shelter starting the fall of 1941, during German bombing. It closed down during the panic that followed the evacuation decree for the people of Moscow: that would be the only time.

Trains parked at platforms could accommodate up to 500,000 people.

During this period, stores and services moved underground; the Kourskaya station housed a library, the Mossoviet held meetings at Mayakovskaya and 217 babies were born throughout the conflict in maternity wards set up in the bowels of the city!

The entrance to the Okhotny Riad station, near the Kremlin. Debuted in 1935, it was renamed Im. Kaganovicha in honor of Lazare Kaganovich from 1955 to 1957, then went back to its original name until 1961 when, this time as a tribute to Karl Marx, it received the appellation Prospekt Marksa, before returning to its original name in 1990!

A subway car in the late 1960s. The interior, which has not changed much over time, is similar to the London subway with its long banquettes facing each other.

↑
Moscow's monorail.
It currently has only one line
dotted with six stations.

tion when it came to decoration. As of 1955, the Moscow subway served as a model for those built in the country's other major cities, such as Leningrad (now St. Petersburg), and in other metropolises of fraternal countries, such as Prague (1974). Today, the network continues to expand. Since 2008, it has been connected to the three Moscow airports via Aeroexpress electric rapid transit trains and a monorail, operated by another company, which connects to two of its lines in the north of the city. In 2015, the subway started a project to replace 3,500 cars and an ambitious development program that, by 2020, should multiply by 1.5 the area covered, thanks to 100 miles (160 km) of new tracks and 60 additional stations. Since progress is valuable only if shared by all, the Moscow subway offers its riders a free Wi-Fi service with no equivalent in the world in both scale and technology, which makes it possible to have service in trains as they move through the tunnels, not only in stations.

An increasingly "connected" network

In 1954, the network had 45 stations, including those of the fourth line, Koltsevaya (from the Russian word for "ring") the circular line that serves seven of the city's nine train stations. In 1953, Stalin's death marked an aesthetic rupture in the subway: the time was still one of reconstruction and the Khrushchev years were those of an inexpensive minimalism both underground and at street level. A decade later, the economic situation was still not really thriving but Leonid Brezhnev, the regime's new strongman revived the earlier tradi-

6.55
MILLION DAILY PASSENGERS

Metro-2: a top-secret network?

→
The prestigious Moscow State University (MGU), also called Lomonosov University, named after the great Russian encyclopedist, is not only the largest and most prestigious higher education establishment in the country. It could also house one of the entrances to a secret network running under the capital.

❝ The Soviets have constructed deep-underground both in urban Moscow and outside the city. These facilities are interconnected by a network of deep interconnected subway lines that provide a quick and secure means of evacuation for the leadership. The leadership can move from their peacetime offices through concealed entryways in protective quarters beneath the city. There are important deep-underground command posts in the Moscow area, one located at the Kremlin. Soviet press has noted the presence of an enormous underground leadership bunker adjacent to Moscow State University. These facilities are intended for the national command authority in wartime. They are estimated to be between 200 m (660 ft) and 300 m (980 ft) deep, and can accommodate an estimated 10,000 people. A special subway line runs from some points in Moscow and possibly to the VIP termi-nal at Vnukovo Airfield (...)" This network, created at the initiative of Stalin, also had entrances from several civilian buildings, including MGU, Moscow State University, in the Ramenki district, and at least two regular subway stations. That is what was revealed in a 1991 report from the U.S. Department of State, with a map to support the claim. Never confirmed or contradicted by the Russian authorities, the existence of this second subway, going by the code name D6, remains a mystery. Spies that defected to the West spoke of it, as did overly talkative subway guards.

→
Joseph Stalin (1878-1953). The "little father of the people" was the uncontested master of the USSR from the late 1920s until his death. It was he who decided to give Moscow a subway and to build a secret network.

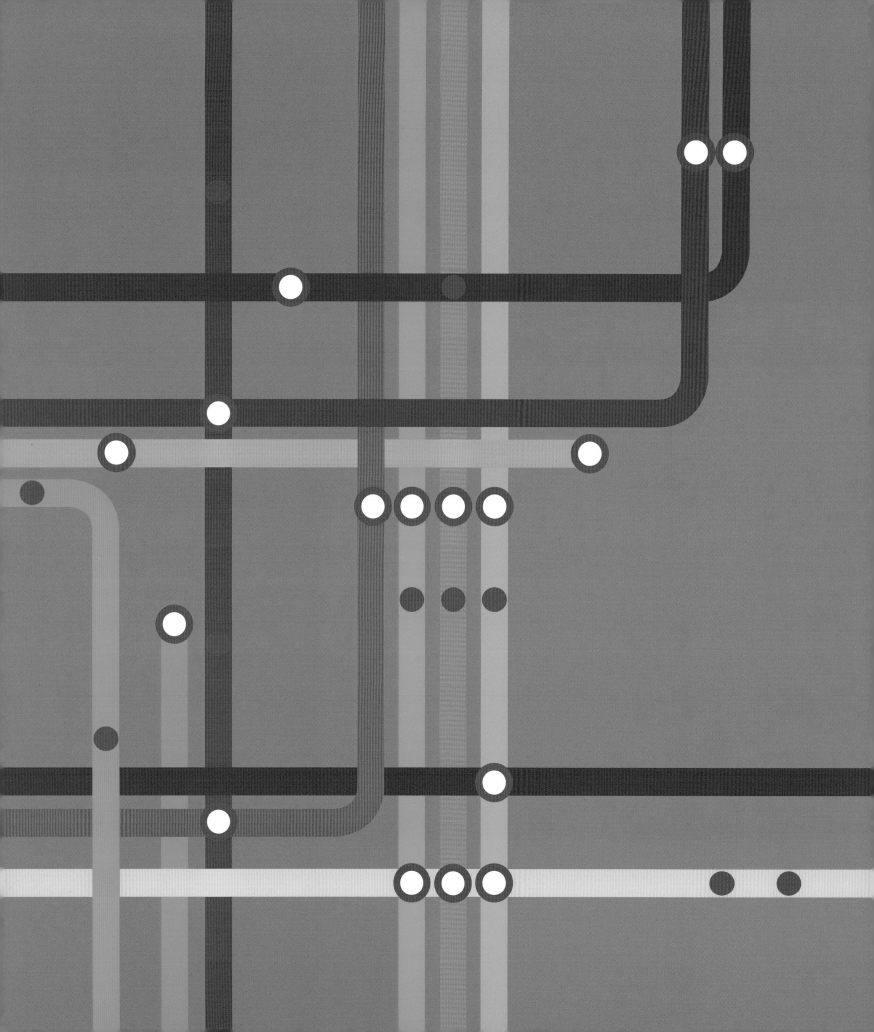

around the world

the most surprising
subway stations

Museum, Toronto, Canada

The platforms of Museum station, opened in 1963, were renovated in 2008. The before and after is quite spectacular! The station's makeover is entirely inspired from the Royal Ontario Museum located nearby and specialized in art, world culture and natural history. The tiled columns now resemble Egyptian deity Osiris or even Toltec warriors.

Elektrozavodskaya, Moscow, Russia

This is one of the stars of the Moscow subway, opened in 1944 and a veritable symbol of the Soviet system at the time. Some 318 incandescent lamps refer to a neighboring electrical plant (hence the station's name). The white marble bas-reliefs pay tribute to the courage of the proletariat during the war. Stalin's pride in this station was so great that it even appears on a 1947 Soviet stamp.

Staromestská , Prague, Czech Republic

Line A of the Prague subway is a succession of stations decorated with the same minimalist principle of cabochon-shaped aluminum panels. Each of them present various colored camaïeu. The alternating concave and convex panels reinforce the impression of movement and speed, creating the optical effect intended by the artist Jaroslav Votruba, in the manner of a work by Vasarely.

Avtovo, Saint Petersburg, Russia

Avtovo truly offers the feeling of entering the tsar's palace: immense chandeliers, bronze plaques, white marble columns and bas-relief ornamentation. But taking a closer look, the tsar has nothing to do with it, since the station is dedicated to the Siege of Leningrad during World War II: a mosaic titled "Victory," picturing a woman and her child, pays tribute to some million civilians who perished in this 900-day ordeal.

Concorde, Paris, France

The Declaration of the Rights of Man and of the Citizen of 1789 is a historical text with a universal reach. And you can read it in its entirety (with one letter per ceramic tile but no spaces between words and no punctuation), and even learn it by heart, thanks to this artwork made by the ceramist Françoise Schein in 1991. The French artist has also decorated stations in Brussels, Lisbon and Berlin.

T-Centralen, Stockholm, Sweden

At the end of the war, the Swedish government started a program to make art more accessible, even by bringing it down into the subway. Stockholm can now brag to be the largest (underground) gallery in the world with more than 90 stations decorated among the 110 on its network. At T-Centralen, you must go down 105 feet (30 m) to admire these floral motifs painted directly on the tunnel's rough walls.

Formosa Boulevard, Kaohsiung, Taiwan

Water, earth, light and fire. These are the themes of the *Dome of Light*, an enormous futuristic glass work imagined for this station by the Italian artist Narcissus Quagliata. An immense kaleidoscope of 4,500 panels, it is the world's largest stained-glass window in a public space to date, measuring 98.4 feet (30 m) in diameter and 23,465 square feet (2,180 sq. m). The station was built for the 2009 world games.

Komsomolskaya, Moscow, Russia

This station, which owes its name to the Komsomol, the Young Communist League, was inspired by a speech of Stalin's given to motivate his troops in 1941. Travelers, however, are plunged into what could be a baroque ballroom: marble balustrades, huge chandeliers and a canary yellow ceiling. Certain of the mosaics evoke great military leaders, heroes of Russian independence.

Cardeal Arcoverde, Rio de Janeiro, Brazil

Ah, Copacabana, its beaches, its rhythms... and its subway station! Named in honor of the first Brazilian cardinal, les Cariocas have nicknamed it "Cardeal Arco-Íris" ("Cardinal Rainbow") because of its multicolored hallways imagined like a chromatic promenade by the architect João Batista Martinez Corrêa. Since then, the city of Rio commissioned him to design a bridge and the Cidade Nova station in 2010.

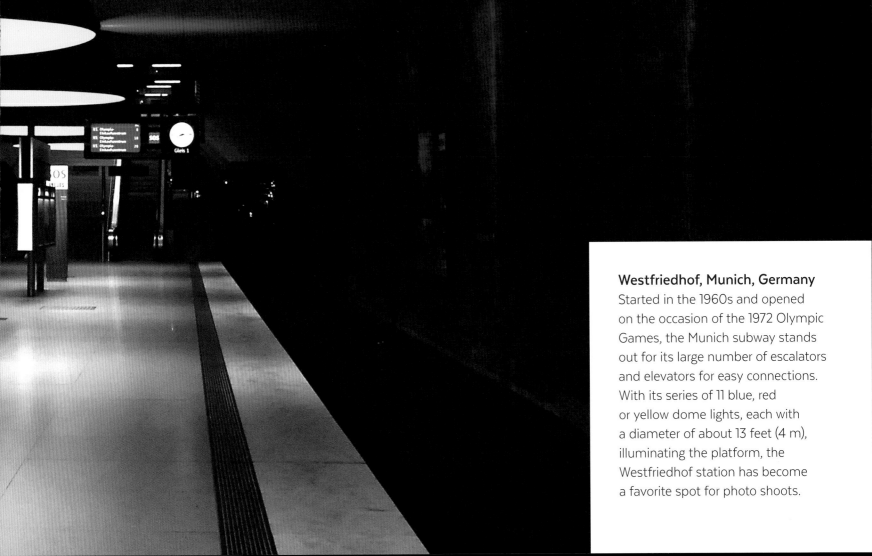

Westfriedhof, Munich, Germany
Started in the 1960s and opened
on the occasion of the 1972 Olympic
Games, the Munich subway stands
out for its large number of escalators
and elevators for easy connections.
With its series of 11 blue, red
or yellow dome lights, each with
a diameter of about 13 feet (4 m),
illuminating the platform, the
Westfriedhof station has become
a favorite spot for photo shoots.

Shinjuku, Tokyo, Japan

Commuters from the west of Tokyo are very familiar with this subway station, connected to the busiest train station in Japan. This is the nerve center of the capital, both underground and at street level. A myriad of corridors and tunnels, over 200 exits... There are plenty of ways to get lost, but the 3.8 million riders who crowd in seem to always find their way, and would not deny the efficiency of the Japanese subway system.

Novoslobodskaya, Moscow, Russia

What Muscovite–supposedly always in a hurry–takes the time to admire the stained-glass windows set into each arch of this station that opened in 1952? And yet, it is around them that the station's architecture took shape. The artist, Pavel Korin, also created a mosaic picturing an allegory of world peace. Originally, a portrait of Stalin was in the place of a dove that we see today.

Münchner Freiheit, Munich, Germany
The futuristic remodeling of one of
Munich's main stations is the fruit of
designer Ingo Maurer: architectural
elements, statues, furnishings, lighting,
the blue and yellow colors... everything
is reflected in the ceiling mirrors and
produces a striking effect of multiplied
space. Playing with perspective, the
recessed lighting of the pillars, gives the
impression that they are lit from within.

Hollywood/Highland, Los Angeles, United States

A few yards below the sidewalk stars of Hollywood Boulevard hides an artistic performance that combines the talents of the sculptress Sheila Klein and the Cannon Design firm. The commission challenged them by imposing the use of standard subway materials when designing this station. The result is a sensual work, especially the metal flowers that house the lighting.

Piccadilly Circus,
London, Great Britain

The famous sound message "Mind the gap" used since 1968, has become a true symbol of the London Underground. However, it remains an important instruction since many subway stations are curved, thus creating a dangerous gap between the train and the platform. On the Piccadilly line, Tim Bentinck's voice, the Australian actor, warns the passengers.

Oriente, Lisbon, Portugal

One of the most important hubs
of the Lisbon subway network, which
can claim to be an architectural work
as magnificent as it is efficient, was
conceived by the Spanish architect
Santiago Calatrava. Subway station,
bus station and train station are
superimposed on six levels. Each of
them houses a creativity that could be
admired by visitors to the Expo '98,
for which this space was created.

丸ノ内線
Marunouchi

Ikebukuro, Tokyo, Japan
Of the 8.5 million Tokyoite travelers who take the subway each day, 2.7 million pass through the Ikebukuro station, a veritable crossroads. To keep things moving, the famous "pushers" wear white gloves as they strive to get as many people as possible into the cars. And during rush hours, some lines reserve cars for women only, helping them stay serene while packed in like sardines.

Marienplatz, Munich, Germany

Located under the new City Hall, Marienplatz is one of the most important stations in Munich, combining railway and subway stations. Necessary extension work led to the construction of this underground passage, designed by the architect Alexander von Branca and conducted with respect for the station's original concept, already clad in orange, deep blue and green tiles.

Wilhelminaplein, Rotterdam, Netherlands

A unique experience awaits you in the 460-foot (140 m) underground passage that connects this station to the Luxor theater. The computer-controlled lighting design gradually changes color every moment, giving travelers the impression that it is following them. Enameled panels are perforated with small holes outlining the silhouettes of children whose families contributed to this project.

Stand on the right

**Canary Wharf, London,
Great Britain**

The English are not without contradictions: the people, who walk to the left in hallways and on platforms, always stay to the right on subway escalators. The practice comes from the design of the first escalators in the early 20th century, which at the time ended diagonally so that riders could put their weight on the right foot in order to get off. The habit has remained.

Capital International Airport, Terminal 3, Beijing, China

The Beijing subway, started in 1965, is the oldest subway in China. But its expansion is meteoric: just between 2007 and 2014, 235 miles (378 km) of tracks were added. Nearly every line is scheduled to be extended in the coming years and several new lines should be created very shortly. By 2020, the city is supposed to have a network of almost 620 miles, (1,000 km) which nearly doubles that of 2015.

Sportivnaya, Saint Petersburg, Russia

The mosaics inspired by the games of ancient Greece, which decorate the platforms of this station opened in 1997, are in sharp contrast to the sleek aluminum and lighting of this long tunnel. It should be mentioned that the hallway, which passes under the Neva and joins Vasilyevsky Island, was not debuted until 2015.

Rådhuset, Stockholm, Sweden

It may be because this station is located where Franciscan monks prayed in the 15th century that the artist Sigvard Olsson shaped it like an underground cave, embellished with imaginary archeological discoveries, such as doors from a medieval palace or the foundations of an immense fireplace. Its red lighting and the rough aspect of its walls give the effect of volcanic magma, typical of organic architecture.

Candidplatz, Munich, Germany

Veritable cathedral of iridescent colors, the station seems to create a constant movement, regularly disturbed by the arrival of the subway trains. The color spectrum goes from red at one end of the platform all the way to blue at the other end. Walls and columns participate in these color changes, making Candidplatz an always new experience for the traveler.

Szent Gellért tér, Budapest, Hungary

One of the world's oldest subways shows that it is thoroughly modern with this station renovated in 2014, including a mosaic décor imagined by the Hungarian artist Tamás Komoróczky. Its spiral patterns are a genuine invitation to an intergalactic trip, as is all of the architecture of this station that combines technical prowess with misleading perspectives and concrete interlacing.

Arts et Métiers, Paris, France

Have you ever been inside a submarine? That's exactly the impression you have in this station decorated in 1994 by François Schuiten. The comic book artist was freely inspired by Jules Verne's famous *Nautilus* to celebrate with machinery gear the bicentenary of the Conservatoire National des Arts et Métiers, a museum devoted to technological progress, served by this station.

Hospital 12 de Octubre, Madrid, Spain

Debuted in 2007, this large Madrid station, serving a hospital, is decorated with a work 180 feet (55 m) long by 16 feet (5 m) high, titled *Humani Corpore*. In a tribute to medicine and the human body, it shows 12 human figures on a background of anatomical reproduction sheets dating from the 19th century. This is a worthwhile way to take shelter from the heat of the Spanish capital...

Toledo, Naples, Italy

Dive into this sparkling ocean designed by several international artists, including William Kentridge. Natural light from the outside enters into these abysses to create bluish reflections, making Toledo one of the most magnificent stations in Europe, although it only opened in September 2012. In spite of its small size, the Neapolitan network is one of the most attractive and spectacular to ride.

Gongguan, Taipei, Taiwan

It's undoubtedly due to its recent construction (the first phase was opened in 1996) that all of the stations of the Taiwan network are accessible to the disabled. Facilities include entrances, elevators and train doors adapted for wheel chairs, along with tactile signs and paths as well as reserved seats in each car. Many of the world's subways could take a lesson from the Taipei network...

Foggy Bottom-GWU, Washington, United States

Like waffles? Then take the Washington subway! Your eyes will have a feast since several of the stations boast a coffered concrete vault whose honeycomb cells evoke the crisp cake. Debuted in 1976, the capital's network is rather monotonous visually and the stations only stand out by the shape of their arches. Nevertheless, many government workers appreciate its punctuality.

191st Street, New York, United States

The tunnels and underground passages of the New York Subway have long been the favorite canvas of graffiti artists and some of them have brought street art to an exceptional level. Since 2008, this 885-foot (270 m) long (art?) gallery located in northern Manhattan has been decorated at the request of the municipality. After having been vandalized, in 2015 six artists, chosen through a competition, took back the walls.

City Hall, New York, United States

Closed since 1945, this station is an architectural marvel with its high vaults covered with tiles and its elegant skylights that let natural light stream through. The ghost station, where time seems to stand still, debuted at the same time as the New York subway, in 1904. Now it can be visited on only very rare occasions.

Wall Street, New York, United States
This station might well be at the feet of the opulent New York Stock Exchange, but like so many others in the city, it is showing its age. It badly needs a facelift, but at the rate things are going, that won't happen until 2067! Half of the budget is still lacking to bring the obsolescent subway network in line with the city's famous modernity.

Jumeirah Lake Towers, Dubaï, United Arab Emirates

At 74 miles (119 km) in length this is the longest automated subway in the world. The network, mainly elevated, circulates in the middle of a forest of towers. The Universal Exposition of 2020 and its expected 25 million visitors is serving as a motor for the lengthening of lines. As in most Muslim countries, a section of the train is reserved for women and children. Comfort is absolute, even if the car is still queen in Dubai.

Puhung, Pyongyang, North Korea
It's the dictatorship's showcase and tourists are obliged to take a ride between the only two authorized stations. There, everything is order and beauty, Communism, allegories and monumental bronzes. This artificialness helps to fuel the rumor that that there is a secret network used only to transport officials. Others say that the subway is only open two hours a day, due to a lack of electricity.

" YOU CAN GO TO A BURLESQUE SHOW.
A COUNTRY BLUE GRASS SHOW AND A
PUNK SHOW ALL IN ONE NIGHT.
WHERE ELSE CAN YOU GET THAT? "

LARONDA

HALEY, ADVERTISING EXECUTIVE

HALEY

World Trade Center, New York, United States

A new station rebuilt after the September 11 attacks, this gigantic hub with a birdlike appearance is named Oculus. It was designed by the Spanish architect Santiago Calatrava. The framework extends underground where riders can bask in the daylight as they take advantage of the many stores that liven up one of the busiest connection centers in Manhattan.

Solna Centrum, Stockholm, Sweden
When the 1970s arrived with their share of protests and revolts, the decoration of the subway was not left behind. The destruction of forest and rural depopulation were denounced on this over 3,000-foot (914 m) long wall, painted by Anders Åberg and Karl-Olav Bjork in 1975. The blood-red sky renders this landscape of forests and traditional houses almost demonic.

Universidad de Chile, Santiago, Chile

Stretching over 12,900 square feet (1,198 sq. m), the majestic mural painted by Mario Toral and titled *Memoria Visual de una Nación* tells the history of Chile in two parts (*Past* and *Present*). From the Spanish conquest to modern times, including Pinochet's dictatorship, this is a veritable museum that can be visited for the price of a subway ticket. And many other stations on this network also give pride of place to artists.

Beitucheng, Beijing, China

Located on the Olympic line that serves many of the capital's monuments, Beitucheng naturally welcomes an increasing number of tourists. They will note echoes of the ancient art of China in the white and blue porcelain seen here in a truly contemporary rendering. Platform pillars, underground exits, and even subway maps are given over to this essential traditional element of Chinese culture.

Vine/Hollywood, Los Angeles, United States

Decidedly, the Hollywood myth goes all the way underground! The Seventh Art serves as the décor: 1930s projectors, ceiling covered with film reels, movie screens framed by curtains. One wall even reproduces the score of the song *Hooray for Hollywood*. The artist Magu is responsible for this glitzy design, with columns disguised as palm trees, but in perfect tune with the mecca of cinema.

Olaias, Lisbon, Portugal

While the rivets that stud the
monumental platform colonnades
evoke the Parisian Arts et Métiers
station, Olaias is much more than
a lookalike. In fact, for Expo '98 Lisbon,
its designers imagined it as a celebration
of "500 years of Portuguese inventions,"
and the use of polychrome elements,
including glass panels, steel sheets
and ceramics make it an artwork
in its own right.

Pyatnitskoye Shosse, Moscow, Russia

Travel further to get closer, that could be the motto of this terminus station, located over 30 miles (48 km) from the center of Moscow. And it is just as far from the ornamentation of the Stalin era. Yet the tradition of innovation and opulence is still there, with white marble walls, black marble pillars, and circles of light on the ceiling that seem to come from nowhere.

Dilworth Park, Philadelphia, United States

The luminous station entrance is the brilliant demonstration of the subway being an integral part of redevelopment of this Philadelphia neighborhood. Access is meant to be as welcoming as possible in this space, modernized in response to the network's expansion. And if you look on the other side, it is like a glass springboard reflecting the surrounding buildings.

Georg-Brauchle-Ring, Munich, Germany

The Great Journey by Franz Ackermann (born 1963) which decorates this station consists of 400 metal panels, alternating monochromes, postcards, paintings and photographs. Thanks to this subjective and colorful mapmaking, riders can create their own journeys each time they pass through the station. It is the ultimate proof that you can be sedentary and a traveler at the same time.

index

A   B

photo credits

AFP
p. 194-195 : Chinas photos/Getty/AFP.

Alamy
p. 37 : Oote Boe/Alamy ; 58 : Steve Kenny/Alamy ; 78 : Zoonar GmbH/Alamy.

All rights reserved
p. 6-7.

Corbis
p. 20, 36 : Corbis ; 126-127 : Stuart Dee/Corbis ; 188-189, 190-191, 192-193 : Sergio J. Pitamitz/Corbis ; 196-197 : Spaces Images/Blend Images/Corbis.

Gamma-Rapho
p. 28, 39, 40 top, 40 bottom, 41, 42, 45, 47, 57 : Keystone-France/Gamma-Rapho ; 30-31 : François Lochon/Gamma-Rapho ; 48-49 : Jean-Louis Swiners/Gamma-Rapho ; 62 : A.D.N.-Bundesarchiv/Gamma ; 87, 89 : Paolo Koch/Rapho ; 88 : Herve Gloaguen/Rapho ; 92 : Ton Koene/Gamma ; 93 : Frederic Berthet/Hoa-Qui/Gamma ; 94 : Eric Lafforgue/Rapho ; 106-107 : Didier Bizet/Gamma-Rapho ; 114 : CameraPress/Gamma.

Getty Images
p. 23 : Gerry Cranham/Fox Photos/Getty Images ; 24-25, 26 : Topical Press Agency/Hulton Archive/Getty Images ; 27 : London Express/Hulton Archive/Getty Images ; 29 : A. J. O'Brien/Fox Photos/Hulton Archive/Getty Images ; 32 : Chris Ware/Getty Images ; 33 : Doug Armand/Getty Images ; 34: Gallo Images/Getty Images ; 50 : Marvin E. Newman/Getty Images ; 54 : FHM/Getty Images ; 64 : Central Press/Getty ; 65 : Stiebing/Ullstein Bild/Getty Images ; 66 : Torsten Andreas Hoffmann/Look-foto/Getty Images ; 67 : Joerg Fockenberg/EyeEm/Getty Images ; 81 : Robert Rosamilio/NY Daily News Archive/Getty

Images ; 113 : Andrey Rudakov/Bloomberg/Getty Images ; 186-187 : Robert Harding World Imagery/Getty Images ; 198-199 : Klaus Rose/Ullstein Bild/Getty Images ; 200-201 : Klaus Rose/Ullstein Bild/Getty Images ; 204-205 : Nick Frank/Photonica World/Getty Images.

Hemis
p. 60-61, 184-185 : Jon Arnold Images/Hemis.

Leemage
p. 56 : Bianchetti/Leemage ; 59 : Artedia/Leemage ; 96 : Gattoni/Leemage ; 100 : Sovfoto/UIG/Leemage ; 105 bottom : ITAR-TASS/UIG/Leemage.

Library of Congress
p. 21 : Graves, C. H./Library of Congress ; 70, 72, 73 : Walter, Marc/Library of Congress ; 80 : Vergara, Camilo J./Library of Congress ; 84 : Tsumekichi, Nogawa/Library of Congress ; 85 : H.C. White Co./Library of Congress ; 98 : Library of Congress.

New York Transit Museum
p. 74 : Courtesy of New York Transit Museum.

Photo12
p. 63 : Photo12/Ullstein Bild.

Roger Viollet
p. 38, 53 : Musée Carnavalet/Roger-Viollet ; 43, 44 : Maurice-Louis Branger/Roger-Viollet ; 52 : Roger-Viollet.

Rue des Archives
p. 22 : Mary Evans/Rue des Archives ; 75 : Alliance/Rue des Archives ; 99, 103, 104, 109, 110, 111 : ITAR-TASS/Rue des Archives.

Shutterstock
Front cover, p. 6-7, 18, 68, 71, 76-77, 78, 79, 51, 82, 90-91, 95, 101, 105 top, 112, 115, 118-119, 120-121, 122-123, 124-125, 128-129, 130-131, 132-133, 134-135, 136-137, 138-139, 140-141, 142-143, 144-145, 146-147, 148-149, 150-151, 152-153, 154-155, 156-157, 158-159, 160-161, 162-163, 164-165, 166-167, 168-169, 170-171, 172-173, 174-175, 176-177, 178-179, 180-181, 182-183, 202-203, back cover..

C